MODERN
SCOTTISH POETRY

MODERN SCOTTISH POETRY

An Anthology
of the Scottish Renaissance

EDITED BY
MAURICE LINDSAY

FABER AND FABER LTD
24 Russell Square
London

First published in mcmxlvi
Second edition, revised and entirely reset,
published in mcmlxvi
Printed in Great Britain
by Ebenezer Baylis and Son, Limited
The Trinity Press, Worcester, and London

THE LITTLE WHITE ROSE

The Rose of all the world is not for me.
I want for my part
Only the little white rose of Scotland
That smells sharp and sweet—and breaks the heart.

HUGH MACDIARMID

CONTENTS

9

11

13

ACKNOWLEDGMENTS

FOR permission to include copyright poems in this anthology, I wish to thank the authors and publishers listed below:

Violet Jacob, *Scottish Poems* (Oliver and Boyd); Pittendrigh MacGillivray, *Bog-Myrtle and Peat Reek*, Miss MacGillivray; John Ferguson, *Thyrea* (Andrew Melrose (1927) Ltd.) and Mrs Ferguson; Marion Angus, *The Turn of the Day*, *Sun and Candlelight* (Faber) and *Selected Poems* (Seriff); Helen B. Cruikshank, *Up the Noran Water* (Methuen); Hugh MacDiarmid, *Sangschaw* and *Pennywheep* (Blackwood), *Scots Unbound* (Aeneas Mackay) and *Collected Poems* (Oliver and Boyd); Alexander Gray, *Gossip* (Faber), *Songs & Ballads from Heine* (Grant Richards) and *Sir Hallwyn* (Oliver and Boyd); Hamish MacLaren, *Sailor with Banjo* (Gollancz); Margot Robert Adamson, *Northern Holiday* (Cobden-Sanderson); Edwin Muir, *Journeys and Places* (Dent) and *Collected Poems* (Faber); Lewis Spence, *Plumes of Time* (Allen and Unwin); Andrew Young, *Collected Poems* (Cape); Muriel Stewart, *Poems* (Heinemann); William Jeffrey, *Sea Glimmer* (Maclellan) and Mrs Jeffrey; William Soutar, *Poems in Scots* (Dakers) and *Collected Poems* (Dakers); Ruthven Todd, *Garland for the Winter Solstice* (Dent) and *The Acreage of the Heart* (Maclellan); Douglas Young, *Auntran Blads* and *A Braird o Thristles* (Maclellan) and the author; J. F. Hendry, *The Bombed Happiness* (Routledge); Sorley Maclean, *Dain Do Eimhir* (Maclellan); Adam Drinan, *The Men on the Rocks* (Fortune Press), *The Ghosts of the Strath* (Maclellan) and the author; G. S. Fraser, *Home Town Elegy* (P. L. Nicholson and Watson) and *The Traveller Has Regrets* (Harvill); W. S. Graham, *Cage Without Grievance* (Parton Press), *2nd Poems* (P. L. Nicholson and Watson) and *The Nightfishing* (Faber); Norman McCaig, *Riding Light*, *The Sinai Sort*, *A Round of Applause* (Chatto and Windus) and the author; Maurice Lindsay, *The Enemies of Love* (Robert Hale), *One Later Day* (Brookside Press) and the author; Sydney Goodsir Smith, *The Deevil's Waltz* (Maclellan), *Figs and Thistles* (Oliver and Boyd) and *So Late into the Night* (Peter Russell); George Campbell Hay, *Fuaran Sleibh* (Maclellan) and *Wind on Loch Fyne* (Oliver and Boyd); William Montgomerie, the author; Robert Garioch, the author, George Bruce, *Sea-Talk*

(Maclellan), *Selected Poems* (Saltire Society and Oliver and Boyd) and the author; Albert D. Mackie, the author; Tom Scott, the author; Robert Maclellan, the author; Donald MacCrae, the author; Sydney Tremayne, *Time and the Wind* (Collins), *The Swans of Berwick* (Chatto and Windus) and the author; Alexander Scott, *The Latest in Elegies* and *Mouth Music* (Caledonian Press); Edwin Morgan, the author; George Mackay Brown, *Loaves and Fishes* (Hogarth) and *The Year of the Whale* (Chatto and Windus); Burns Singer, *Still and All* (Secker and Warburg); W. Price Turner, *The Flying Corset* (Villiers); Alastair Reid, *Oddments, Inklings, Omens and Moments* (Dent) and *Passwords* (Weidenfeld and Nicolson); Iain Crichton Smith, *Thistles and Roses* and *The Law and the Grace* (Eyre and Spottiswoode); Ian H. Finlay, *The Dancers Inherit the Party* (Migrant Press); Stewart Conn, the author; Robin Fulton, the author; D. M. Black, the author.

Every effort has been made to try to trace the executors of the poets no longer living. Should anyone have been inadvertently omitted, or any other copyright owner denied rightful acknowledgment, I trust that my apologies will be accepted

The Scots translations by Hugh MacDiarmid of George Campbell Hay's two Gaelic poems, were made specially for the first edition of this anthology. When it was being compiled, Douglas Young made many helpful suggestions. Similar kind assistance has been given to me on this occasion by George Bruce and by Alexander Scott. I should also like to put on record my gratitude to my wife, who typed out the text of the poems.

PREFACE

WHEN I was putting together the first edition of this anthology in the middle of a war, I tried to define my aim: 'to make *Modern Scottish Poetry* a representative culling of the best fruits of the first twenty-five years of the Scottish Renaissance'. In the Preface to that edition, I suggested that since many of the poets were still young, 'the anthology which covers the next quarter may be even better'. Many of the poets originally included are, indeed, represented here by more mature work. Several young writers have added their measure to the harvest of the twentieth-century Scottish Renaissance.

This title, bestowed by a Frenchman, has touched off a great deal of that sterile, bitter controversy in which my compatriots seem both to delight and to excel. Originally, it implied close association with efforts to revive and strengthen Lallans and Gaelic. During the past twenty years, however, it has taken on a wider significance. Few young writers of any consequence today employ Lallans. Every new census reveals a further decline in the number of those who speak, let alone read, the Gaelic. Yet the work of the half-century or so which this anthology celebrates, reflects a variety of experience and an integrity of expression which enable it to stand comparison with the output of any previous period of Scottish literature. These qualities, and not the question of which of Scotland's three languages her writers choose to use, are what constitute the real Scottish Renaissance. As Alexander Scott aptly puts it in his essay 'Scots in English':

'The medium which a Scottish writer uses is, of course, the one to which he is led by personal experience, and it is pointless for propagandists on behalf of any one language to proclaim that the literary use of that language – and that one alone – is a matter of principle. In literature, the poets and the prose-writers make the principles, not vice-versa.'

Every anthologist necessarily exposes himself to the critics' armchair game of 'He should have done this, not that'. I have produced an anthology of the poetry of the Scottish Renaissance which has given me pleasure, and all of which has, for me, a certain memorability. As in the case of the earlier edition, the poets are presented, not strictly in chronological order, but more or less in the order in which they came before the public, an arrangement which seems to me to produce the most satisfactory internal balance.

Hugh MacDiarmid ranks, with Burns and Dunbar, as one of Scotland's three greatest poets. Most of his later poems, however, are extremely long, and it is therefore really impossible to represent adequately the work of his last phase in an anthology which seeks also to be widely representative. Happily, however, his *Collected Poems* is now published. Nor have I felt able to include such long poems as Sydney Goodsir Smith's 'Under the Eildon Tree', Burns Singer's 'The Transparent Prisoner', or Iain Crichton Smith's 'Deer in the High Hills', which together would themselves make up a sizeable volume.

The war verse which appeared in the previous edition has mostly disappeared, since it did not transcend the occasion that called it forth. I have not included 'pop', beat, poster or concrete verse, not only because whatever examples I might have chosen would have been squarely out-of-date by the time the book appeared, but because much of it seems to me to be simply a play-about with typography which, however interesting visually, is in no way memorable as poetry.

I hope very much that those who read *Modern Scottish Poetry* will share my pleasure in the making of it. Collectively, what these poems seem to offer, in the most exciting and permanent manner possible, is a sense of twentieth-century Scotland.

What do you mean when you speak of Scotland?
  The grey defeats that are dead and gone
behind the legends each generation
  savours afresh, yet can't live on?

Lowland farms with their broad acres
  peopling crops? The colder earth
of the clean North East? Or Highland mountains
  shouldering up their rocky dearth?

The rusty clang of spent rivers
  bearing new ships from worn-out flanks?
Kirk spires, once heaven's magnets
  drawing grim praise and unearned thanks?

Black workers in mines and foundries
  shaping the earth to strength and ease?
White workers who shrink or widen
  all human possibilities?

Inheritance of guilt that our country
  has never stood where we feel she should?
The nagging threat of unfinished struggle
  somehow forever lost in the blood?

Scotland's a sense of change, an endless
  becoming for which there was never a kind
of wholeness or ultimate category.
  Scotland's an attitude of mind!

May 1965   MAURICE LINDSAY

VIOLET JACOB

The Water Hen

As I gaed doon by the twa mill dams i' the mornin'
The water-hen cam' oot like a passin' wraith,
And her voice ran through the reeds wi' a sound of warnin',
   'Faith–keep faith!'
'Aye, bird, tho' ye see but ane ye may cry on baith!'

As I gaed doon the field when the dew was lyin',
My ain love stood whaur the road an' the mill-lade met,
And it seemed to me that the rowin' wheel was cryin',
   'Forgie–forget,
And turn, man, turn, for ye ken that ye lo'e her yet!'

As I gaed doon the road 'twas a weary meetin',
For the ill words said yestreen they were aye the same,
And my het he'rt drouned the wheel wi' its heavy beatin'.
   'Lass, think shame,
It's not for me to speak, for it's you to blame!'

As I gaed doon by the toon when the day was springin'
The Baltic brigs lay thick by the soundin' quay
And the riggin' hummed wi' the sang that the wind was singin',
   'Free–gang free,
For there's mony a load on shore may be skailed at sea!'

When I cam hame wi' the thrang o' the years ahint me
There was naucht to see for the weeds and the lade in spate,
But the water-hen by the dam she seemed aye to mind me,
   Cryin' 'Hope–wait!'
'Aye, bird, but my een grow dim, an' it's late – late!'

Tam I' The Kirk

O Jean, my Jean, when the bell ca's the congregation
O'er valley an' hill wi' the ding frae its iron mou',
When a'body's thochts is set on their ain salvation,
   Mine's set on you.

There's a reid rose lies on the Buik o' the Word afore ye
That was growin' braw on its bush at the keek o' day,
But the lad that pu'd yon flower i' the mornin's glory—
   He canna pray.

He canna pray, but there's nane i' the kirk will heed him
Whaur he sits sae still his lane at the side o' the wa',
For nane but the reid rose kens what my lassie gied him—
   It and us twa.

He canna sing for the sang that his ain he'rt raises,
He canna see for the mist that's afore his e'en,
And a voice drouns the hale o' the psalms an' the paraphrases,
   Crying 'Jean! Jean! Jean!'

The Neep-Fields by the Sea

Ye'd wonder foo the seasons rin
This side o' Tweed an' Tyne;
The hairst's awa'; October month
Cam in a whilie syne,
But the stooks are oot in Scotland yet,
There's green upon the tree,
And oh! what grand's the smell ye'll get
Frae the neep-fields by the sea!

The lang lift lies abune the warld,
On ilka windless day
The ships creep doon the ocean line

Sma' on the band o' grey;
And the lang sigh heaved upon the sand
Comes pechin' up tae me
And speils the cliffs tae whaur ye stand
I' the neep-fields by the sea.

Oh, time's aye slow, tho' time gangs fast
When siller's a' tae mak',
An' deith, afore ma poke is fu'
May grip me i' the back;
But ye'll tak ma banes an' my Sawbath braws,
Gin deith's ower smairt for me,
And set them up amang the shaws
I' the lang rows plantit atween the wa's,
A tattie-dulie for fleggin' craws
I' the neep-fields by the sea.

The Wild Geese

'Oh, tell me what was on yer road, ye roarin' norlan' wind
As ye cam' blawin' frae the land that's niver frae my mind?
My feet they trayvel England, but I'm deein' for the north—'
'My man, I heard the siller tides rin up the Firth o' Forth.'

'Aye, Wind, I ken them well eneuch, and fine they fa' and rise,
And fain I'd feel the creepin' mist on yonder shore that lies,
But tell me, ere ye passed them by, what saw ye on the way?'
'My man, I rocked the rovin' gulls that sail abune the Tay.'

'But saw ye naethin', leein' Wind, afore ye cam' to Fife?
There's muckle lyin' yont the Tay that's mair to me nor life.'
'My man, I swept the Angus braes ye haena trod for years—'
'O Wind, forgie a hameless loon that canna see for tears!—'

'And far abune the Angus straths I saw the wild geese flee,
A lang, lang skein o' beatin' wings wi' their heids towards the sea,
And aye their cryin' voices trailed ahint them on the air –'
'O Wind, hae maircy, haud yer whisht, for I daurna listen mair!'

PITTENDRIGH MACGILLIVRAY

Mercy O' Gode

I

Twa bodachs, I mind, had a threep ae day,
   Aboot man's chief end–
   Aboot man's chief end.
Whan the t'ane lookit sweet his words war sour,
Whan the tither leuch out his words gied a clour,
But whilk got the better I wasna sure–
   I wasna sure,
   An' needna say.

II

But I mind them well for a queer-like pair–
   A gangrel kind,
   A gangrel kind:
The heid o' the ane was beld as an egg,
The ither, puir man, had a timmer leg,
An' baith for the bite could dae nocht but beg
   Nocht but beg–
   Or live on air!

III

On a table-stane in the auld Kirkyaird,
   They ca' 'The Houff',
   They ca' 'The Houff',

They sat in their rags like wearyfu' craws,
An' fankl't themsel's about a 'FIRST CAUSE',
An' the job the Lord had made o' His laws,
   Made o' his Laws,
   In human regaird.

IV

Twa broken auld men wi' little but jaw—
   Faur better awa
   Aye—better awa;
Yawmerin' owr things that nane can tell,
The yin for a Heaven, the ither for Hell;
Wi' nae mair in tune than a crackit bell—
   A crackit bell,
   Atween the twa.

V

Dour badly he barkit in praise o' the Lord—
   'The pooer o' Gode
   An' the wull o' Gode';
But Stumpie believ't nor in Gode nor man—
Thocht life but a fecht without ony plan,
An' the best nae mair nor a flash i' the pan—
   A flash i' the pan,
   In darkness smored.

VI

Twa dune men—naither bite nor bed!—
   A sair-like thing—
   An' unco thing.
To the Houff they cam to lay their heid
An' seek a nicht's rest wi' the sleepin' deid,
Whar the stanes wudna grudge nor ony tak' heed
   Nor ony tak' heed:
   But it's ill to read.

VII

They may hae been bitter, an' dour, an' warsh,
  But wha could blame—
    Aye—wha could blame?
I kent bi their look they war no' that bad
But jist ill dune bi an' driven half mad:
What there's nae touch o' kindness this life's owr sad
  This life's owr sad,
    An' faur owr harsh.

VIII

But as nicht drave on I had needs tak' the road,
  Fell gled o' ma dog—
    The love o' a dog:
An' tho nane wad hae me that day at the fair,
I raither't the hill for a houff than in there,
'Neth a table-stane, on a deid man's lair—
  A deid man's lair—
    Mercy o' Gode.

JOHN FERGUSON

A Cock Crowing in a Poulterer's Shop

He will not see the East catch fire again,
  Nor watch the darkening of the drowsy West,
  Nor sniff the morning air with joyous zest,
Nor lead his wives along the grassy lane.

Cooped in a crate, he claps his wings in vain,
  Then hangs his crimson head upon his breast;
  Tomorrow's sun will see him plucked and dressed,
One of a ghastly row of feathered slain.

O chanticleer, I cannot bear it more;
  That crow of anguish, pitiful and stark,
    Makes my flesh quail at thy unhappy lot—
The selfsame cry with which thine ancestor
  Emptied his soul into the tragic dark
    The night that Peter said, 'I know Him not.'

MARION ANGUS

Mary's Song

I wad ha'e gi'en him my lips tae kiss,
Had I been his, had I been his;
Barley breid and elder wine,
Had I been his as he is mine.

The wanderin' bee it seeks the rose;
Tae the lochan's bosom the burnie goes;
The grey bird cries at evenin's fa',
'My luve, my fair one, come awa'.'

My beloved sall ha'e this he'rt tae break,
Reid, reid wine and the barley cake,
A he'rt tae break, an' a mou' tae kiss,
Tho' he be nae mine, as I am his.

Alas! Poor Queen

She was skilled in music and the dance
And the old arts of love
At the court of the poisoned rose
And the perfumed glove,
And gave her beautiful hand
To the pale Dauphin
A triple crown to win—

29

And she loved little dogs
  And parrots
  And red-legged partridges
And the golden fishes of the Duc de Guise
And a pigeon with a blue ruff
She had from Monsieur d'Elboeuf.

Master John Knox was no friend to her;
She spoke him soft and kind,
Her honeyed words were Satan's lure
The unwary soul to bind.
'Good sir, doth a lissome shape
And a comely face
Offend your God His Grace
Whose Wisdom maketh these
Golden fishes of the Duc de Guise?'

She rode through Liddesdale with a song;
'Ye streams sae wondrous strang,
Oh, mak' me a wrack as I come back
But spare me as I gang.'
While a hill-bird cried and cried
Like a spirit lost
By the grey storm-wind tost.

Consider the way she had to go,
Think of the hungry snare,
The net she herself had woven,
Aware or unaware,
Of the dancing feet grown still,
The blinded eyes—
Queens should be cold and wise,
And she loved little things,
  Parrots
  And red-legged partridges
And the golden fishes of the Duc de Guise
And the pigeon with the blue ruff
She had from Monsieur d'Elboeuf.

Think Lang

Lassie, think lang, think lang,
Ere his step comes ower the hill.
Luve gi'es wi' a lauch an' a sang,
An' whiles for nocht but ill.

Thir's weary time tae rue
In the lea-lang nicht yer lane
The ghaist o' a kiss on yer mou'
An' sough o' win' in the rain.

Lassie, think lang, think lang,
The trees is clappin' their han's,
The burnie clatterin' wi' sang
Rins ower the blossomy lan's.

Luve gi'es wi' a lauch an' a sang,
His fit fa's licht on the dew.
Oh, lass, are ye thinkin' lang,
Star een an' honey mou'?

The Lilt

Jean Gordon is weaving a' her lane
Twinin' the threid wi' a thocht o' her ain,
Hearin' the tune o' the bairns at play
That they're singin' amang them ilka day;
And saftly, saftly, ower the hill
Comes the sma', sma' rain.

Aye, she minds o' a simmer's nicht
Afore the waning o' the licht—
Bairnies chantin' in Lover's Lane
The sang that comes ower an' ower again,
And a young lass stealin' awa' to the hill,
In the sma', sma' rain.

31

Oh! lass, your lips were flamin' reid,
An' cauld, mist drops lay on yer heid,
Ye didna gaither yon rose yer lane
And yer he'rt was singin' a sang o' its ain,
As ye slippit hameward, ower the hill,
In the sma', sma' rain.

Jean Gordon, she minds as she sits her lane,
O' a' the years that's bye and gane,
And naething gi'en and a'thing ta'en
But yon nicht o' nichts on the smoory hill
In the sma', sma' rain –
And the bairns are singin' at their play
The lilt that they're liltin' ilka day.

Cotton Grasses

Where seldom footstep passes
  By the lone lochan's edge,
  Foam-white above the sedge,
I hear the cotton grasses –

Whispering, whispering, whispering,
  Now summer days are long,
  The burden of a song
Too sorrowful for singing;

Of joyful tears unwept,
  Of tenderness unwist,
  Of lovers' lips unkissed
And promised trysts unkept.

Where seldom footstep passes,
  So bleak the heath and bare,
  In a cold scentless air
The whispering cotton grasses.

Anemones, they say, are out
  By sheltered woodland streams,
With budding branches all about
  Where Spring-time sunshine gleams;

Such are the haunts they love, but I
  With swift remembrance see
Anemones beneath a sky
  Of cold austerity –

Pale flowers too faint for winds so chill
  And with too fair a name–
That day I lingered on a hill
  For one who never came.

HELEN B. CRUICKSHANK

Shy Geordie

Up the Noran Water,
In by Inglismaddy,
Annie's got a bairnie
That hasna got a daddy.
Some say it's Tammas's
And some say it's Chay's;
An' naebody expec'it it,
Wi' Annie's quiet ways.

Up the Noran Water,
The bonnie little mannie
Is dandlit an' cuddlit close
By Inglismaddy's Annie.
Wha the bairnie's faither is
The lassie never says;

But some think it's Tammas's,
And some think it's Chay's.

Up the Noran Water,
The country folk are kind;
An' wha the bairnie's daddy is
They dinna muckle mind.
But oh! the bairn at Annie's breist,
The love in Annie's e'e'!
They mak' me wish wi' a' my micht
The lucky lad was me!

LEWIS SPENCE

The Queen's Bath-House, Holyrood

Time that has dinged doun castels and hie toures,
And cast great crouns like tinsel in the fire,
That halds his hand for palace nor for byre,
Stands sweir at this, the oe of Venus' boures.
Not Time himself can dwall withouten floures,
Though aiks maun fa' the rose sall bide entire;
So sall this diamant of a queen's desire
Outflourish all the stanes that Time devours.
Mony a strength his turret-heid sall tine
Ere this sall fa' whare a queen lay in wine,
Whose lamp was her ain lily flesh and star.
The walls of luve the mair triumphant are
Gif luve were waesome habiting that place;
Luve has maist years that has a murning face.

34

Portrait of Mary Stuart, Holyrood

Wauken be nicht, and bydand on some boon,
　Glamour of saul, or spirituall grace,
　I haf seen sancts and angels in the face,
And like a fere of seraphy the moon;
But in nae mirk nor sun-apparelled noon
　Nor pleasance of the planets in their place
　Of luve devine haf seen sae pure a trace
As in yon shadow of the Scottis croun.

Die not, O rose, dispitefull of hir mouth,
　Nor be ye lillies waeful at hir snaw;
　　This dim devyce is but hir painted sake,
The mirour of ane star of vivand youth,
　That not hir velvets nor hir balas braw
　　Can oueradorn, or luve mair luvely make.

ALEXANDER GRAY

Scotland

Here in the uplands
The soil is ungrateful;
The fields, red with sorrel,
Are stony and bare.
A few trees, wind-twisted—
Or are they but bushes?—
Stand stubbornly guarding
A home here and there.

Scooped out like a saucer,
The land lies before me;
The waters, once scattered,
Flow orderedly now
Through fields where the ghosts

Of the marsh and the moorland
Stll ride the old marches,
Despising the plough.

The marsh and the moorland
Are not to be banished;
The bracken and heather,
The glory of broom,
Usurp all the balks
And the fields' broken fringes,
And claim from the sower
Their portion of room.

This is my country,
The land that begat me.
These windy spaces
Are surely my own,
And those who here toil
In the sweat of their faces
Are flesh of my flesh,
And bone of my bone.

Hard is the day's task–
Scotland, stern Mother!–
Wherewith at all times
Thy sons have been faced–
Labour by day,
And scant rest in the gloaming,
With Want an attendant,
Not lightly outpaced.

Yet do thy children
Honour and love thee.
Harsh is thy schooling,
Yet great is the gain:
True hearts and strong limbs,
The beauty of faces,
Kissed by the wind
And caressed by the rain.

Heine in Scots

There were three kings cam frae the East;
They spiered in ilka clachan:
'O, which is the wey to Bethlehem,
My bairns, sae bonnily lachin'?'

O neither young nor auld could tell;
They trailed till their feet were weary.
They followed a bonny gowden starn,
That shone in the lift sae cheery.

The starn stude ower the ale-hoose byre
Whaur the stable gear was hingin'.
The owsen mooed, the bairnie grat,
The kings begoud their singin'.

On a Cat, Ageing

He blinks upon the hearth-rug,
    And yawns in deep content,
Accepting all the comforts
    That Providence has sent.

Louder he purrs and louder,
    In one glad hymn of praise
For all the night's adventures,
    For quiet restful days.

Life will go on for ever,
    With all that cat can wish;
Warmth and the glad procession
    Of fish and milk and fish.

Only – the thought disturbs him –
He's noticed once or twice,
The times are somehow breeding
A nimbler race of mice.

The Fine Fechtin Moose
(after the Dutch)

'Twas gettin geyan late at e'en,
When I daundered doon the street my lane;
And the mune was sheenin murkily,
   Ay, ay, ay, murkily.
There was ne'er a starn to be seen.

'Fairest o' fair, O, hear my cry;
O, open and let your love inby;
Sae lang have I been here standin,
   Ay, ay, ay, standin,
That I'm frozen all-utterly.'

'Deed, and I winna open to ye,
Nor to ony gangrel, as weel ye may be;
But first, you maun tell me strauchtly,
   Ay, ay, ay, strauchtly,
That there's nane that you lo'e but me'.

'Dear lass, I lo'e you; weel you ken
That you've aye been the only ane.
But sae lang have I been here standin,
   Ay, ay, ay, standin,
That I'm frozen cauld to the bane.'

In the nicht, in the nicht, in the middle o' the nicht,
A dunt at the winnock gae's baith a fricht.
And her mither, O ay, *she* heard it,
   Ay, ay, ay, SHE heard it:
'Are you sure, Jean, that a' thing's a' richt?'

'O mither, it's only Baudrons, the cat:
He's after a moose, and that's what he's at;
And dod, but he's grippit the beastie;
    Ay, ay, ay, the beastie–
She's a fine fechtin moose for a' that!

The Deil o' Bogie
(after the German)

When I was young, and ower young,
I wad a deid-auld wife;
But ere three days had gane by,
    Gi-Ga-Gane-by,
I rued the sturt and strife.

Sae to the Kirk-yaird furth I fared,
And to the Deil I prayed:
'O, muckle Deil o' Bogie,
    Bi-Ba-Bogie,
Come, tak the runkled jade.'

When I got hame, the soor auld bitch
Was deid, ay, deid eneugh.
I yokkit the mare to the dung-cairt,
    Ding-Dang-Dung-cairt,
And drove her furth–and leuch!

And when I cam to the place o' peace,
The grave was howked, and snod:
'Gae canny wi' the corp, lads,
    Ci-Ca-Corp, lads,
You'll wauk her up, by God!

Ram in, ram in the bonnie yird
Upon the ill-daein wife.
When she was hale and herty,
    Hi-Ha-Herty,
She plagued me o' my life.'

But when I gat me hame again,
The hoose seemed toom and wide.
For juist three days I waited,
    Wit-Wat-Waited,
Syne took a braw young bride.

In three short days my braw young wife
Had ta'en to lounderin me.
'Gie's back, dear Deil o' Bogie,
    Bi-Ba-Bogie,
My auld calamitie!'

ANDREW YOUNG

Loch Brandy

All day I heard the water talk
From dripping rock to rock
And water in bright snowflakes scatter
On boulders of the black Whitewater;
But louder now than these
The silent scream of the loose tumbling screes.

Grey wave on grey stone hits
And grey moth flits
Moth after moth, but oh,
What floats into that silver glow,
What golden moth
That rises with a strange majestic sloth?

O heart, why temble with desire
As on the water shakes that bridge of fire?
The gold moth floats away, too soon
To narrow to a hard white moon
That scarce will light the path
Stumbling to where the cold mist wreaths the strath.

The Mountain

The burn ran blacker for the snow
And ice-floe on ice-floe
Jangled in heavy lurches
Beneath the claret-coloured birches.

Dark grouse rose becking from the ground
And deer turned sharp heads round,
The antlers on their brows
Like stunted trees with withered boughs.

I climbed to where the mountain sloped
And long wan bubbles groped
Under the ice's cover,
A bridge that groaned as I crossed over.

I reached the mist, brighter than day,
That showed a specious way
By narrow crumbling shelves,
Where rocks grew larger than themselves.

But when I saw the mountain's spire
Looming through that damp fire,
I left it still unwon
And climbed down to the setting sun.

The Paps of Jura

Before I crossed the sound
  I saw how from the sea
These breasts rise soft and round,
  Not two but three;

Now, climbing, I clasp rocks
  Storm-shattered and sharp-edged,

Grey ptarmigan their flocks,
  With starved moss wedged;

And mist like hair hangs over
  One barren breast and me,
Who climb, a desperate lover,
  With hand and knee.

The Echoing Cliff

White gulls that sit and float,
Each on his shadow like a boat,
Sandpipers, oystercatchers
And herons, those grey stilted watchers,
From loch and corran rise,
And as they scream and squawk abuse
Echo from wooded cliff replies
So clearly that the dark pine boughs,
Where goldcrests flit
And owls in drowsy wisdom sit,
Are filled with sea-birds and their cries.

EDWIN MUIR

Robert the Bruce Stricken with Leprosy: to Douglas

'My life is done, yet all remains,
  The breath has vanished, the image not,
The furious shapes once forged in heat
  Love on, though now no longer hot.

'Steadily the shining swords
  In order rise, in order fall,
In order on the beaten field
  The faithful trumpets call.

'The women weeping for the dead
    Now are not sad but dutiful,
The dead men stiffening in their place
    Proclaim the ancient rule.

'Great Wallace's body hewn in four,
    So altered, stays as it must be.
O Douglas, do not leave me now.
    For by your side I see

'My dagger sheathed in Comyn's heart,
    And nothing there to praise or blame,
Nothing but order which must be
    Itself and still the same.

'But that Christ hung upon the Cross,
    Comyn would rot until Time's end
And bury my sin in boundless dust,
    For there is no amend

'In order; yet in order run
    All things by unreturning ways.
If Christ live not, nothing is there
    For sorrow or for praise.'

So the King spoke to Douglas once
    A little time before his death,
Having outfaced three English kings
    And kept a people's faith.

Mary Stuart

My brother Jamie lost me all,
Fell cleverly to make me fall,
And with a sure reluctant hand
Stole my life and took my land.

It was jealousy of the womb
That let me in and shut him out,
Honesty, kingship, all shut out,
While I enjoyed the royal room.

My father, was his, but not my mother,
We were, yet were not, sister, brother,
To reach my mother he had to strike
Me down and leap that deadly dyke.

Over the wall I watched him move
At ease through all the guarded grove,
Then hack, and hack, and hack it down,
Until that ruin was his own.

Scotland, 1941

We were a family, a tribe, a people,
Wallace and Bruce guard now a painted field,
And all may read the folio of our fable,
Peruse the sword, the sceptre and the shield.
A simple sky roofed in that rustic day,
The busy corn-fields and the haunted holms,
The green path winding up the ferny brae.
But Knox and Melville clapped their preaching palms
And huddled all the harvest gold away,
Hoodicrow Peden in the blighted corn
Hacked with his rusty beak the starving haulms.
Out of that desolation we were born.

Courage beyond the point and obdurate pride
Gave us a nation, robbed us of a nation.
Defiance absolute, and myriad-eyed
That could not pluck the palm plucked our damnation.
We with such courage and the bitter wit
To fell the ancient oak of loyalty,

And strip the peopled hill and the altar bare,
And crush the poet with an iron text,
How could we read our souls and learn to be?

A pallid drove of faces harsh and vexed,
We watch our cities burning in their pit,
To salve our souls grinding dull lucre out,
We, fanatics of the frustrate and the half,
Who once set Purgatory Hill in doubt.
Now smoke and dearth and money everywhere,
Grim heirlooms of each fainter generation,
And mummied housegods in their musty niches,
Burns and Scott, sham bards of a sham nation,
And spiritual defeat wrapped warm in riches,
No pride but pride of pelf. Long since the young
Died in great bloody battles to carve out
This towering pulpit of the Golden Calf.
Montrose, Mackail, Argyll, perverse and brave,
Twisted the stream, unhooped the ancestral hill.
Never had Dee or Don or Yarrow or Till
Huddled such thriftless honour in a grave.

If we could raise those bones so brave and wrong,
Revive our ancient body, part by part.
We'd touch to pity the annalist's iron tongue
And gather a nation in our sorrowful heart.

Then

There were no men and women then at all,
But bone grinding on bone,
And angry shadows fighting on a wall
That now and then sent out a groan
Mingled with lime and stone,
And sweated now and then like tortured wood
Big drops that looked yet did not look like blood.

And yet as each drop came a shadow faded
And left the wall.
There was a lull.
Until another in its shadow arrayed it,
Came, fought and left a blood-mark on the wall.
And that was all: the blood was all.

If women had been there they would have wept
To see the blood, unowned, unwanted,
Poor as forgotten script.
The wall was haunted
By mute maternal presences whose sighing
Fluttered the fighting shadows and shook the wall
As if that fury of death itself were dying.

The Sufficient Place

See, all the silver roads wind in, lead in
To this still place like evening. See, they came
Like messengers bearing gifts to this little house,
And this great hill worn down to a patient mound,
And these tall trees whose motionless branches bear
An aeon's summer foliage, leaves so thick
They seem to have robbed a world of shade, and kept
No room for all these birds that line the boughs
With heavier riches, leaf and bird and leaf.
Within the doorway stand
Two figures, Man and Woman, simple and clear
As a child's first images. Their manners are
Such as were known before the earliest fashion
Taught the Heavens guile. The room inside is like
A thought that needed thus much space to write on,
Thus much, no more. Here all's sufficient. None
That comes complains, and all the world comes here,
Comes, and goes out again, and comes again.
This is the Pattern, these the Prototypes,

Sufficient, strong and peaceful. All outside
From end to end of the world is tumult. Yet
These roads to not turn in here but writhe on
Round the wild earth for ever. If a man
Should chance to find this place three times in Time
His eyes are changed and make a summer silence
Amid the tumult, seeing the roads wind in
To their still home, the house and the leaves and birds.

The Little General

Early in spring the little General came
Across the sound, bringing the island death,
And suddenly a place without a name,
And like the pious ritual of a faith,

Hunter and quarry in the boundless trap,
The white smoke curling from the silver gun,
The feather curling in the hunter's cap,
And clouds of feathers floating in the sun,

While down the birds came in a deafening shower,
Wing-hurricane, and the cattle fled in fear.
Up on the hill a remnant of a tower
Had watched that single scene for many a year,

Weaving a wordless tale where all were gathered
(Hunter and quarry and watcher and fabulous field),
A sylvan war half human and half feathered,
Perennial emblem painted on the shield

Held up to cow a never-conquered land
Fast in the little General's fragile hand.

A Birthday

I never felt so much
Since I have felt at all
The tingling smell and touch
Of dogrose and sweet briar,
Nettles against the wall,
All sours and sweets that grow
Together or apart
In hedge or marsh or ditch.
I gather to my heart
Beast, insect, flower, earth, water, fire,
In absolute desire,
As fifty years ago.

Acceptance, gratitude:
The first look and the last
When all between has passed
Restore ingenuous good
That seeks no personal end,
Nor strives to mar or mend.
Before I touched the food
Sweetness ensnared my tongue;
Before I saw the wood
I loved each nook and bend,
The track going right and wrong;
Before I took the road
Direction ravished my soul.
Now that I can discern
It whole or almost whole,
Acceptance and gratitude
Like travellers return
And stand where they first stood.

HUGH MACDIARMID

The Bonnie Broukit Bairn
(For Peggy)

Mars is braw in crammasy,
Venus in a green silk goun,
The auld mune shak's her gowden feathers,
Their starry talk's a wheen o' blethers,
Nane for thee a thochtie sparin',
Earth, thou bonnie broukit bairn!
—But greet, an' in your tears ye'll droun
The haill clanjamfrie!

The Eemis-Stane

I' the how-dumb-deid o the cauld hairst nicht
The warl like an eemis-stane
Wags i the lift;
An my eerie memories fa'
Like a yowdendrift.

Like a yowdendrift so's I couldna read
The words cut oot i the stane
Had the fug o fame
An history's hazelraw
No' yirdit thaim.

Empty Vessel

I met ayont the cairney
A lass wi tousie hair
Singin til a bairnie
That was nae longer there.

Wunds wi warlds tae swing
Dinna sing sae sweet.
The licht that bends owre aathing
Is less taen up wi't.

An Apprentice Angel
(To L. M. W.)

I

Try on your wings; I ken vera weel
It wadna look seemly if ony ane saw
A Glasgow Divine ga'en flutherin' aboot
In his study like a drunk craw.

But it 'ud look waur if you'd to bide
In an awkward squad for a month or mair
Learnin' to flee afore you could join
Heaven's air gymnkhana aince you got there.

Try on your wings, and gi'e a bit flap,
Pot belly and a', what does it maitter?
Seriously prepare for your future state
—Tho' that's never been in your natur'!

II

As the dragonfly's hideous larva creeps
Oot o' the ditch whaur it was spawned
And straight is turned to the splendid fly,
Nae doot by Death's belated hand

You'll be changed in a similar way,
But as frae that livin' flash o' licht
The cruel features and crawlin' legs

50

O' its former state never vanish quite
I fancy your Presbyterian Heaven
'Ll be haunted tae wi' a hellish leaven.

From *Second Hymn to Lenin*

Lo! A Child is Born

I thought of a house where the stones seemed suddenly changed
And became instinct with hope, hope as solid as themselves.
And the atmosphere warm with that lovely heat,
The warmth of tenderness and longing souls, the smiling anxiety
That rules a home where a child is about to be born.
The walls were full of ears. All voices were lowered.
Only the mother had the right to groan or complain.
Then I thought of the whole world. Who cares for its travail
And seeks to encompass it in like lovingkindness and peace?
There is a monstrous din of the sterile who contribute nothing
To the great end in view, and the future fumbles,
A bad birth, not like the child in that gracious home
Heard in the quietness turning in its mother's womb,
A strategic mind already, seeking the best way
To present himself to life, and at last, resolved,
Springing into history quivering like a fish,
Dropping into the world like a ripe fruit in due time.—
But where is the Past to which Time, smiling through her tears
At her new-born son, can turn crying: 'I love you?'

Milk-wort and Bog-cotton

Cwa' een like milk-wort and bog-cotton hair!
I love you, earth, in this mood best o' a'
When the shy spirit like a laich wind moves
And frae the lift nae shadow can fa'
Since there's nocht left to thraw a shadow there
Owre een like milk-wort and milk-white cotton hair.

Wad that nae leaf upon anither wheeled
A shadow either and nae root need dern
In sacrifice to let sic beauty be!
But deep surroondin' darkness I discern
Is aye the price o' licht. Wad licht revealed
Naething but you, and nicht nocht else concealed.

The Watergaw

Ae weet forenicht i' the yow-trummle
I saw yon antrin thing,
A watergaw wi' its chitterin' licht
Ayont the on-ding;
An' I thocht o' the last wild look ye gied
Afore ye dee'd!

There was nae reek i' the laverock's hoose
That nicht—an' nane i' mine;
But I hae thocht o' that foolish licht
Ever sin syne;
An' I think that mebbe at last I ken
What your look meant then.

From *Second Hymn to Lenin*

Oh, it's nonsense, nonsense,
Nonsense at this time o' day
That breid-and-butter problems
S'ud be in ony man's way.

They s'ud be like the tails we tint
On leaving the monkey stage;
A' maist folk fash aboot's alike
Primaeval to oor age.

We're grown-up folk that haena yet
Put bairnly things aside
—A' that's material and moral—
And oor new state descried.

Sport, love, and parentage,
Trade, politics, and law
S'ud be nae mair to us than braith
We hardly ken we draw.

Freein' oor poo'ers for greater things,
And feg's there's plenty o' them,
Tho' wha's still trammelt in alow
Canna be tenty o' them—

With the Herring Fishers

'I see herrin'.'—I hear the glad cry
And 'gainst the moon see ilka blue jowl
In turn as the fishermen haul on the nets
And sing: 'Come, shove in your heids and growl.'

'Soom on, bonnie herrin', soom on,' they shout,
Or 'Come in, O come in, and see me,'
'Come gie the auld man something to dae.
It'll be a braw change frae the sea.'

O it's ane o' the bonniest sichts in the warld
To watch the herrin' come walkin' on board
In the wee sma' 'oors o' a simmer's mornin'
As if o' their ain accord.

For this is the way that God sees life,
The haill jing-bang o's appearin'
Up owre frae the edge o' naethingness
—It's his happy cries I'm hearin'.

'Left, right—O come in and see me,'
Reid and yellow and black and white
Toddlin' up into Heaven thegither
At peep o' day frae the endless night.

'I see herrin',' I hear his glad cry,
And 'gainst the moon see his muckle blue jowl,
As he handles buoy-tow and bush raip
Singin': 'Come, shove in your heids and growl!'

Two Memories

Religion? Huh! Whenever I hear the word
It brings two memories back to my mind.
Choose between them and tell me which
You think the better model for mankind.

Fresh blood scares sleeping cows worse than anything else on earth.
An unseen rider leans far out from his horse with a freshly-skinned
Weaner's hide in his hands, turning and twisting the hairy slimy
    thing
And throwing the blood abroad on the wind.

A brilliant flash of lightning crashes into the heavens.
It reveals the earth in a strange yellow-green light,
Alluring yet repelling, that distorts the immediate foreground
And makes the gray and remote distance odious to the sight.

And a great mass of wraithlike objects on the bed ground
Seems to upheave, to move, to rise, to fold and undulate
In a wavelike mobility that extends to an alarming distance.
The cows have ceased to rest: they are getting to their feet.

Another flash of lightning shows a fantastic and fearsome vision.
Like the branches of some enormous grotesque sprawling plant
A forest of long horns waves, and countless faces
Turn into the air, unspeakably weird and gaunt.

54

The stroke of white fire is reflected back
To the heavens from thousands of bulging eyeballs,
And into the heart of any man who sees
This diabolical mirroring of the lightning numbing fear falls.

Is such a stampede your idea for the human race?
Haven't we milled in it long enough? My second memory
Is of a flight of wild swans. Glorious white birds in the blue October
    heights
Over the surly unrest of the ocean! Their passing is more than
    music to me
And from their wings descends, and in my heart triumphantly peels
The old loveliness of earth that both affirms and heals.

The Glass of Pure Water

'In the de-oxidisation and re-oxidisation of hydrogen in a single
drop of water we have before us, truly, so far as force is concerned,
an epitome of the whole life. . . . The burning of coal to move an
iron wheel differs only in detail, and not in essence, from the
decomposition of a muscle to effect its own concentration.'
                                        —JAMES HINTON.

'We must remember that his analysis was done not intellectually,
but by an immediate process of intuition; that he was able, as it
were, to taste the hydrogen and oxygen in his glass of water,'
                        —ALDOUS HUXLEY (of D. H. Lawrence)

'Praise of pure water is common in Gaelic poetry.'
                    —W. J. WATSON: 'Bardachd Ghaidhlig.'

Hold a glass of pure water to the eye of the sun!
It is difficult to tell the one from the other
Save by the tiny hardly visible trembling of the water.
This is the nearest analogy to the essence of human life
Which is even more difficult to see.

Dismiss anything you can see more easily;
It is not alive–it is not worth seeing.
There is a minute indescribable difference
Between one glass of pure water and another
With slightly different chemical constituents.
The difference between one human life and another
Is no greater; colour does not colour the water:
You cannot tell a white man's life from a black man's.
But the lives of these particular slum people
I am chiefly concerned with, like the lives of all
The world's poorest, remind me less
Of a glass of water held between my eyes and the sun
–They remind me of the feeling they had
Who saw Sacco and Vanzetti in the death cell
On the eve of their execution.
–One is talking to God.

I dreamt last night that I saw one of His angels
Making his centennial report to the Recording Angel
On the condition of human life.
Look at the ridge of skin between your thumb and forefinger.
Look at the delicate lines on it and how they change
–How many different things they can express–
As you move out or close in your forefinger and thumb.
And look at the changing shapes–the countless
Little gestures, little miracles of line–
Of your forefinger and thumb as you move them.
And remember how much a hand can express,
How a single slight movement of it can say more
Than millions of words–dropped hand, clenched fist,
Snapping fingers, thumb up, thumb down,
Raised in blessing, clutched in passion, begging,
Welcome, dismissal, prayer, applause,
And a million other signs, too slight, too subtle,
Too packed with meaning for words to describe,
A universal language understood by all.
And the Angel's report on human life
Was the subtlest movement–just like that–and no more;

A hundred years of life on the Earth
Summed up, not a detail missed or wrongly assessed,
In that little inconceivably intricate movement.

The only communication between man and man
That says anything worth hearing
—The hidden well-water; the finger of destiny;—
Moves as that water, that angel, moved.
Truth is the rarest thing and life
The gentlest, most unobtrusive movement in the world.
I cannot speak to you of the poor people of all the world
But among the people in these nearest slums I know
This infinitesimal twinkling, this delicate play
Of tiny signs that not only say more
Than all speech, but all there is to say,
All there is to say and to know and to be.
There alone I seldom find anything else,
Each in himself or herself a dramatic whole,
An 'agon' whose validity is timeless.
Our duty is to free that water, to make these gestures,
To help humanity to shed all else,
All that stands between any life and the sun,
The quintessence of any life and the sun;
To still all sound save that talking to God;
To end all movements save movements like these.
India had that great opportunity centuries ago
And India lost it—and became a vast morass,
Where no water wins free; a monstrous jungle
Of useless movement; a babel
Of stupid voices, drowning the still small voice.
It is our turn now; the call is to the Celt.

This little country can overcome the whole world of wrong
As the Lacadaemonians the armies of Persia.
Cornwall—Gaeldom—must stand for the ending
Of the essential immorality of any man controlling
Any other—for the ending of all Government
Since all Government is a monopoly of violence;

For the striking of this water out of the rock of Capitalism;
For the complete emergence from the pollution and fog
With which the hellish interests of private property
In land, machinery, and credit
Have corrupted and concealed from the sun,
From the gestures of truth, from the voice of God,
Hundreds upon hundreds of millions of men,
Denied the life and liberty to which they were born
And fobbed off with a horrible travesty instead
—Self righteous, sunk in the belief that they are human,
When not a tenth of one per cent show a single gleam
Of the life that is in them under their accretions of filth.

And until that day comes every true man's place
Is to reject all else and be with the lowest
The poorest—in the bottom of that deepest of wells
In which alone is truth; in which
Is truth only—truth that should shine like the sun,
With a monopoly of movement, and a sound like talking to God....

DONALD SINCLAIR

Sligh Nan Seann Seun

Saoibhir sith nan sian an nochd air Tìr-an-Àigh.
Is ciùine ciùil nam fiath ag iadhadh Innse Gràidh,
Is èasgaidh gach sgiath air fianlach dian an Dàin
Is slighe nan seann seun a' siaradh siar gun tàmh.
Saoibhir com nan cruach le cuimhne làithean aosd',
Sona gnùis nan cuan am bruadair uair a dh'aom;
Soillseach gach uair an aigne suaimhneach ghaoth—
O, làithean mo luaidh, 'ur n-uaill, 'ur n-uails', 'ur gaol!
O, làithean geala gràidh le'r gnàthan geala còir,
O, aimsirean an àigh le'r gàire, gean, is ceòl—
O, shaoghail nan gràs nan gathan aithne 's eoil,
C'uime thréig 's nach d'fhàg ach àilte àin 'ur glòir?

58

An ioghnadh deòin is dùil bhi dol an null 'nur déidh,
Ri ionndruinn nan rùn a lìon 'ur sgùird le spéis?
An ioghnadh ceòl nan dùl bhi seinn air cliù 'ur réim'
Is fabhra crom gach sùl bhi tais fo dhùbhradh leug?
A làithean sin a thriall le ial-luchd àis mo shluaigh,
C'uime thàrr 'ur miann gach dias a b'fhiachmhor buaidh?
An ioghnadh an iarmailt shiar bhi nochd fo shnuadh,
'S 'ur n-àrosan an cian bhi laist le lias bith-bhuan?
An ioghnadh lom gach làir bhi luaidh air làn 'ur sgàeòil?
An ioghnadh cnuic is ràdh a' chomha-thràth 'nam beòil?
An ioghnadh cruit nan dàn bhi bìth fo sgàil' a neòil–
Is ealaidh-ghuth nam bàrd gun seun, gun sàire seòil?
Chan ioghnadh cill mo shluaigh an cois nan cuan bhi balbh,
Chan ioghnadh uchd nan tuam bhi'n tòic le luach na dh'fhalbh,
O, shaoghail, is truagh nach till aon uair a shearg,
'S nach tàrr mo dheòin, ge buan, aon fhios á suain nam marbh!

The Path of the Old Spells
from the Gaelic of Donald Sinclair
(Scots version by Hugh MacDiarmid)

Rich is the peace o' the elements the nicht owre the Land o' Joy
And rich the evenness o' the calm's music roond the Isles o' Love,
Ilka wing plies urgently in obedience to nature
While the path o' the auld spells winds inexorably westwards.
Rich the breist o' the hills wi' memories o' bygone days,
Serene the face o' the seas wi' dreams o' the times that are gane.
O seilfu' days, your pride, your noblesness, your love!
O white days o' love wi' your clean and kindly ways!
O times o' joy wi' your lauchter, your cheer, and your music!
O warld o' grace, lit by rays o' knowledge and art!
Why ha'e you gane and left hardly a trace o' the noontide o' your
  glory?
Is it a wonder desire and hope seek to follow eftir you,
Fain for the secret that aince cled your lap wi' esteem?
Is it a wonder the elements sing o' your time and poo'er

And the curved lid o' ilka eye is weak frae the fire o' jewels?

O yon days that ha'e gane wi' the shinin' load o' the wisdom o' my
race,

Why did you want to strip awa' ilka last ear o' maist worthy
excellence?

Nae wonder the western lift is noo sae illustrious wi' licht

And that your dwellin's in the distance are alowe wi' an everlasting
flame!

Nae wonder the bareness o' ilka flat bespeaks the fullness o' your
story!

Nae wonder the hills haud the words o' twilicht in their mooths!

Nae wonder the harp o' the sangs is silent under the belly o' yon
clood

And the voice-of-song o' the bards without spell or excellence o'
art!

Nae wonder the kirkyaird o' my folk, by the sea, is dumb!

Nae wonder the breists o' the graves are a' hoven wi' the worth o'
what's gane!

O Warld! It is a woe that no' an 'oor that has gane can ever come
back,

Nor can my desire, tho' lastin', draw a single word frae the sleep
o' the deid!

HAMISH MACLAREN

Island Rose

She has given all her beauty to the water;
    She has told her secrets to the tidal bell;
And her hair is a moon-drawn net, and it has caught her,
    And her voice is in the hollow shell.

She will not come back any more now, nor waken
    Out of her island dream where no wind blows:
And only in the small house of the shell, forsaken,
    Sings the dark one whose face is a rose.

ALBERT D. MACKIE

Molecatcher

Strampin' the bent, like the Angel o' Daith,
    The mowdie-man staves by;
Alang his pad the mowdie-worps
    Like sma' Assyrians lie.

And where the Angel o' Daith has been,
    Yirked oot o' their yirdy hames,
Lie Sennacherib's blasted hosts
    Wi' guts dung oot o' wames.

Sma' black tramorts wi' gruntles grey,
    Sma' weak weemin's han's,
Sma' bead-een that wid touch ilk hert
    Binnae the mowdie-man's.

MARGOT ROBERT ADAMSON

Edinburgh

If they should ask what makes the stuff of us
We should call up such idle things and gone!
The theatre we knew in Grindley Street,
The midnight bell vibrating in the Tron.

A church tower's clock along the Lothian Road,
Whose face lit up would turn a lemon moon,
Seen o'er the pallid bleakness of the street
In the chill dusks that harry northern June,

A Sunday morning over Samson's Ribs,
The smoky grass that grows on Arthur's Seat;
Turned-yellow willow leaves in Dalkeith Road,
Dropt lanceheads on the pavement at our feet;

Glimpses got sometimes of the Forfar hills
With the white snows upon them, or, maybe,
Green waters washing round the piers of Leith
With all the straws and flotsam of the sea.

A certain railway bridge whence one can look
On a network of bright lines and feel the stress,
Tossing its plumes of milky snow, where goes
Loud in full pace the thundering North Express

Behind its great green engine; or in Spring
Black-heaved the Castle Rock and there where blows
By Gordon's window wild the wallflower still,
The gold that keeps the footprints of Montrose.

The Pentlands over yellow stubble fields
Seen out beyond Craigmillar, and the flight
Of seagulls wheeling round the dark-shared plough,
Strewing the landscape with a rush of white.

Such idle things! Gold birches by hill lochs,
The gales that beat the Lothian shores in strife,
The day you found the great blue alkanette,
And all the farmlands by the shores of Fife.

MURIEL STEWART

The Seed Shop

Here in a quiet and dusty room they lie,
  Faded as crumbled stone or shifting sand,
Forlorn as ashes, shrivelled, scentless, dry,
  Meadows and gardens running through my hand.

Dead that shall quicken at the trump of Spring,
  Sleepers to stir beneath June's splendid kiss,
Though birds pass over, unremembering,
  And no bee seek here roses that were his.

In this brown husk a dale of hawthorn dreams,
  A cedar in this narrow cell is thrust
That will drink deeply of a century's streams;
  These lilies shall make Summer on my dust.

Here in their safe and simple house of death,
  Sealed in their shells a million roses leap;
Here I can blow a garden with my breath,
  And in my hand a forest lies asleep.

In the Orchard

'I thought you loved me.'
                'No, it was only fun.'
'When we stood there, closer than all?'
                        'Well, the harvest **moon**

Was shining and queer in your hair, and it turned my head.'
'That made you?'
        'Yes.'
                'Just the moon and the light it made
Under the tree?'
            'Well, your mouth too.'
                    'Yes. My mouth?'
'And the quiet there that sang like the drum in the booth.
You shouldn't have danced like that.'
                  'Like what?'
                      'So close,
With your head turned up, and the flower in your hair, a rose
That smelt all warm.'
           'I loved you. I thought you knew
I wouldn't have danced like that with any but you.'
'I didn't know. I thought you knew it was fun.'
'I thought it was love you meant.'
                'Well, it's done. '
                    'Yes, it's done
I've seen boys stone a blackbird, and watched them drown
A kitten . . . it clawed at the reeds, and they pushed it down
Into the pool while it screamed. Is that fun, too?'
'Well, boys are like that . . . your brothers . . .'
                    'Yes, I know.
But you, so lovely and strong! Not you! Not you!'
'They don't understand it's cruel. It's only a game.'
'And are girls fun, too?'
            'No. Still in a way it's the same.
It's queer and lovely to have a girl . . .'
                'Go on.'
'It makes you mad for a bit to feel she's your own,
And you laugh and kiss her, and maybe you give her a ring,
But it's only in fun.'
            'But I gave you everything.'
'Well, you shouldn't have done it. You know what a fellow thinks
When a girl does that.'
            'Yes, talks of her over his drinks
And call her a—'

'Stop that now. I thought you knew.'
'But it wasn't with anyone else. It was only you.'
'How did I know? I thought you wanted it too.
I thought you were like the rest—Well, what's to be done?'
'To be done?'
                          'Is it all right?'
                                    'Yes.'
                                          'Sure?'
                                                'Yes, but why?'
'I don't know. I thought you were going to cry.
You said you had something to tell me.'
                                    'Yes, I know.
It wasn't anything really . . . I think I'll go,'
'Yes, it's late. There's thunder about, a drop of rain
Fell on my hand in the dark. I'll see you again
At the dance next week. You're sure that everything's right?'
'Yes.'
        'Well, I'll be going.'
                          'Kiss me . . .'
                                    'Good night . . .'
                                          'Good night.'

WILLIAM JEFFREY

Native Element

A cloud walking.
    Thus a child had said
Watching the landward progress of a swan
Emerge in drip of silver from a pond,
Questing sweet roots and grasses succulent.

And as the bird advanced with serpent head
Elatedly he seemed to entertain
The self-same thought. But almost instantly
His cumber'd carriage and his weighted bones

Dissuaded him. A thousand ages bent
Their arc on him. The brontosaurus moved
In his deliberate web-footed gait:
He was the essence of ungainliness.

Returned now. Oxen-wise in reeds he knelt,
And thrusting forth the snowdrift of his breast
Upon the silver water fell to rest,
At one again with his own element.

Now all the lissomness of wind and wave
Was gathered in his beauty and his pride,
No hint of any clumsiness was there,
But all was poised to perfect functioning.
He paused, and shook the glory of each wing,
And then in stillness glided on, within
His sky the sole majestic Jupiter.

WILLIAM SOUTAR

The Gowk

Half doun the hill where fa's the linn,
    Far frae the flaught of fowk,
I saw upon a lanely whin,
    A lanely singin' gowk!
     Cuckoo, cuckoo;
Behind my back
The howie hill stuid up and spak,
     Cuckoo, cuckoo.

There was nae soun', the loupin' linn
    Was frostit in its fa';
Nae bird was on the lanely whin
    Sae white with fleurs o' snaw.
     Cuckoo, cuckoo;

I stuid stane still
And gently spak the howie hill
   Cuckoo, cuckoo.

The Tryst

O luely, luely, cam she in
And luely she lay doun:
I kent her be her caller lips
And her breists sae sma' and roun'.

A' thru the nicht we spak nae word
Nor sinder'd bane frae bane:
A' thru the nicht I heard her hert
Gang soundin' wi' my ain.

It was about the waukrife hour
When cocks begin to craw
That she smool'd saftly thru the mirk
Afore the day wud daw.

Sae luely, luely, cam she in
Sae luely was she gaen;
And wi' her a' my simmer days
Like they had never been.

The Thocht

Young Janie was a strappin' lass
   Wha deed in jizzen-bed,
And monie a thocht her lover thocht
   Lang eftir she was dead;

But aye, wi' a' he brocht to mind
    O' misery and wrang,
There was a gledness gathered in
    Like the owrecome o' a sang:

And, gin the deid are naethingness
    Or they be minded on
As hinny to a hungry ghaist
    Maun be a thocht like yon.

Wait for the Hour
(*to a poet*)

When day follows inarticulate day;
When the mind would speak
But the heart has nought to say—
Wait for the hour.
Wait for the hour
Nor fret against the sense
Which is more old, more wise than intelligence.
O thrust not forth your word
Like a driven bird
Which braves its fledgeling breast to the blasts of the air;
Which strains an awkward wing
To meet the spring
While yet the fields are broken and the boughs are bare.
Wait for the hour;
As, hoarded within the bud,
The leaves must wait if they would bear a flower;
As wait earth's waters till their strength can flood
Under the moon.
Wait for the hour:
It is not late nor soon,
But this your power—
To curb the fretful brain and trust the blood.

Miracle

Summer
Is on the hill;
But in the moveless air
The fountain of the hawthorn hangs
With frost.

The Thocht

As the minister prayed wi' hands in air
He had the dreid thocht that he was bare:
That his goun and a' his ither claes
Were huggerin doun ablow his knees.

But he wudna daur unsteek his e'en
To see what mebbe his fowk had seen—
That, waur nor John Baptist frae the waste,
He stüde mither-naked like a beast.

Sae ablow the prayer that soundit abüne
He slippit in twa, three words o' his ain—
That heids were doun, and e'en were ticht,
And afore he was düne a' wud be richt.

Wi' as guid a grace as he cud fend
He brocht his petition to its end:
Gowkit to see gin he was douce—
And, the Lord be thankit, sae he was.

The Lanely Mune

Saftly, saftly, through the mirk
the mune walks a' hersel:
ayont the brae; abune the kirk;
and owre the dunnlin bell.
I wudna be the mune at night
for a' her gowd and a' her licht.

Song

Whaur yon broken brig hings owre;
Whaur yon water maks nae soun';
Babylon blaws by in stour:
Gang doun wi' a sang, gang doun.

Deep, owre deep, for onie drouth:
Wan eneuch an ye wud droun:
Saut, or seelfu', for the mouth;
Gang doun wi' a sang, gang doun.

Babylon blaws by in stour
Whaur yon water maks nae soun':
Darkness is your only door;
Gang doun wi' a sang, gang doun.

WILLIAM MONTGOMERIE

Elegy

(for William Soutar)

A narrowing of knowledge to one window to a door
Swinging inward on a man in a windless room
On a man inwardly singing
                            on a singing child

Alone and never alone a lonely child
Singing
          in a mirror dancing to a dancing child
Memory sang and words in a mimic dance
Old words were young and a child sang.

A narrowing of knowledge to one room to a doorway
To a door in a wall swinging bringing him friends
A narrowing knowledge to
                              an arrow in bone in the marrow
An arrow
          death
                    strung on the string of the spine.

To the live crystal in the palm and the five fingers
To the slow thirty years' pearl in the hand
Shelled in a skull in the live face of a statue
Sea-flowered on the neck of broken marble
Sunken fourteen years in that aquarium.

RUTHVEN TODD

From *In Edinburgh 1940*

I was born in this city of grey stone and bitter wind,
Of tenements sooted up with lying history:
This place where dry minds grow crusts of hate, as rocks
Grow lichens. I went to school over the high bridge
Fringed with spikes which, curiously, repel the suicides;
And I slept opposite the rock-garden where the survivors,
Who had left Irving and Mallory under the sheet of snow,
Planted the incarvillea and saxifrages of the Himalayas.

And, as I grew in childhood, I learned the knack to slip
The breech-block of the field-gun in the park, peering
Along the rifled barrel I would enclose a small circle

71

Of my world, marked out for death; death as unreal
As the gun's forgotten action under the hot African sun.
Growing older, I met other and more frequent ghosts,
Lying to preserve the remnants of a reputation.

Knox spoke sweetly in the Canongate–'I was not cruel
To gaunt Mary, the whore denying the hand that lit the fuse.'
Charles Stuart returned, alive only to the past, his venture
That was little but a dream, forgetting the squat bottle,
Quivered in the lace-veined hand and the unseeing sharpness of his
     eyes.
Bruce could not stir the cobwebs from his skeleton,
And the editor spoke regretfully, but firmly, of poor Keats.

Here the boy Rimbaud paused, flying love and lust,
Unnoticed on his journey to the Abyssinian plains
And the thick dropsy of his tender leg. Here the other Knox,
Surgeon and anatomist, saw the beauty of the young girl
Smothered by Burke and Hare. And here, O certainly,
God was the private property of a chosen few
Whose lives ran carefully and correctly to the grave.

This, deny it as I like, is still my city and these ghosts,
Sneer as I may, have helped to make me what I am.
A woman cried in labour and Simpson inhaled his vapour
Falling, anaesthetized, across the drawing-room table.
John Graham, laird of Claverhouse, did not have tears
For those he killed, nor did the silver bullet weep for him.
This city, bulwark of the east, formed me as I am.

In September, 1937

Coming in September, through the thin streets,
I thought back to another year I knew,
Autumn, lifting potatoes and stacking peats
On Mull, while the Atlantic's murky blue
Swung sluggishly in past Jura, and the hills
Were brown lions, crouched to meet the autumn gales.

In the hard rain and the rip of thunder,
I remember the haze coming in from the sea
And the clatter of Gaelic voices by the breakwater,
Or in the fields as the reapers took their tea;
I remembered the cast foal lying where it died,
Which we buried, one evening, above high tide:

And the three rams that smashed the fank-gate,
Running loose for five days on the moor
Before we could catch them—far too late
To prevent an early lambing the next year.
But these seemed out of place beside the chip-shop
And the cockney voices grumbling in the pub.

In September, I saw the drab newsposters
Telling of wars, in Spain and in the East,
And wished I'd stayed on Mull, their gestures
Frightened me and made me feel the unwanted guest,
The burden on the house who having taken salt
Could never be ejected, however grave his fault.

In September, we lit the fire and talked together,
Discussing the trivialities of a spent day
And what we would eat. I forgot the weather
And the dull streets and the sun on Islay,
And all my fear. I lost my carefully-kept count
Of the ticks to death, and, in September, was content.

Northwards the Islands

Northwards the islands and the sullen shore,
The bald rocks where sulk the summer seas;
Distantly, as in a shell held to the ear,
I can remember their petulant noise
Quickening in winter to a sullen roar.

The leisurely seal fishing from the rock
And the otter trapped beside the burn,
The silver sand with network of brown wrack,
Were once my life, but I cannot return
To scythe the corn or build a stack.

The difference has grown in me,
The islands stay the same. No change
Is possible for me, who move so quickly
To strengthen my acquaintance with the strange.
Tomorrow someone else, but 'I' today.

Where I am going and where I will end
Do not concern me for the present.
Nostalgia for the past I have, and find
It is the immincence of the future I resent,
Not my romantic leanings to the land.

Personal History: For My Son

O my heart is the unlucky heir of the ages
And my body is unwillingly the secret agent
Of my ancestors; those content with their wages
From history: the Cumberland Quaker whose gentle
Face was framed with lank hair to hide the ears
Cropped as a punishment for his steadfast faith,
The Spanish lady who had seen the pitch lake's broth
In the West Indian island, and the Fife farmers
To whom the felted barley meant a winter's want.

My face presents my history, and its sallow skin
Is parchment for the Edinburgh lawyer's deed:
To have and hold in trust, as feoffee therein
Until such date as the owner shall have need
Thereof. My brown eyes are jewels I cannot pawn,
And my long lip once curled beside an Irish bog,

My son's whorled ear was once my father's, then mine;
I am the map of a campaign, each ancestor has his flag
Marking an advance or a retreat. I am their seed.

As I write I look at the five fingers of my hand,
Each with its core of nacre bone, and rippled nails;
Turn to the palm and the traced unequal lines that end
In death—only at the tips my ancestry fails—
The dotted swirls are original and are my own:
Look at this fringed polyp which I daily use
And ask its history, ask to what grave abuse
It has been put: perhaps it curled about the stone
Of Cain. At least it has known much of evil.

And perhaps as much of good, been tender
When tenderness was needed, and been firm
On occasion, and in its past been free of gender,
Been the hand of a mother holding the warm
Impress of the child against her throbbing breast,
Been cool to the head inflamed in fever,
Sweet and direct in contact with a lover.
O in its cupped and fluted shell lies all the past;
My fingers close about the crash of history's storm.

In the tent of night I hear the voice of Calvin
Expending his hatred of the world in icy winds;
Man less than red ant beneath the towering mountain,
And God a troll more fearful than the feudal lords;
The Hugenots in me, flying Saint Bartholomew's Day,
Are in agreement with all this, and their resentful hate
Flames brighter than the candles on an altar, the grey
Afternoon is lit by Catherine wheels of terror, the street
Drinks blood, and pity is death before their swords.

The cantilever of my bones acknowledges the architect,
My father, to whom always the world was a mystery
Concealed in the humped base of a bottle, one solid fact
To set against the curled pages and the tears of history.

I am a Border keep, a croft and a solicitor's office,
A country rectory, a farm and a drawing board:
In me, as in so many, the past has stowed its miser's hoard,
Won who knows where nor with what loaded dice.
When my blood pulses it is their blood I feel hurry.

These forged me, the latest link in a fertile chain,
With ends that run so far that my short sight
Cannot follow them, nor can my weak memory claim
Acquaintance with the earliest shackle. In my height
And breadth I hold my history, and then my son
Holds my history in his small body and the history of another,
Who for me has no contact but that of flesh, his mother.
What I make now I make, indeed, from the unknown,
A blind man spinning furiously in the web of night.

Watching You Walk

Watching you walk slowly across a stage,
Suddenly I am become aware of all the past;
Of all the tragic maids and queens of every age,
Of Joan, whose love the flames could not arrest.

Of those to whom always love was the first duty,
Who saw behind the crooked world the ugly and weak,
Whose kindliness was no gesture; no condescending pity
Could rule their actions; those whom Time broke,

But whom he could not totally destroy.
Hearing the truth you give to these dead words,
Whose writer feared the life they might enjoy,
I can recall the mating orchestra of birds

Behind your voice, as lying by the lake,
You read me Owen, and I, too deeply moved,
Watched the swans for a moment, before I spoke
The trivialities, unable to tell you how I loved.

Watching your fingers curl about a painted death,
I am suddenly glad that it is April, that you are queen
Of all the sordid marches of my bruised heart,
That, loving you, the poplars never seemed to green.

Glad of my lonely walk beside the shrunken river,
Thinking of you while seeing the tufts of ash,
The chestnut candles and unreal magnolia's wax flower;
Glad that, in loving you, the whole world lives afresh.

To A Very Beautiful Lady

And when you walk the world lifts up its head,
Planets are haloed by the unembarrassed stars,
The town lies fallow at your feet, the ancient dead
Recall their loves, their queens and emperors,
Their shepherds and the quiet pastoral scene.
For less than you Troy burned and Egypt fell,
The corn was blasted while it still stood green,
And Faustus went protesting into Hell.

Be careful, sweet, adored by half the world,
Time to its darlings is not always kind,
There lie the lovelies whom the years have scored
Deeper than all the hearts which once repined.
The knife you hold could cut an empire low
Or in your own breast place the suicidal blow.

GEORGE CAMPBELL HAY

Bisearta

Chì mi ré geard na h-oidhche
dreòs air chrith 'na fhroidhneas thall air fàire,
ag clapail le a sgiathaibh,
a'sgapadh s ag ciaradh rionnagan na h-àird' ud.

Shaoileadh tu gu'n cluinnte,
ge cian, o 'bhuillsgein ochanaich no caoineadh
ràn corruich no gàir fuatha,
comhart chon cuthaich uaith no ulfhairt fhaolchon,
gu'n ruigeadh drannd an fhòirneirt
o'n fhùirneis òmair iomall fhéin an tsaoghail;
ach sud a' dol an leud e
ri oir an speur an tosdachd olc is aognuidh.

C'ainm an nochd a th'orra,
na sràidean bochda anns an sgeith gach uinneag
a lasraichean s a deatach,
a sradagan is sgreadail a luchd thuinidh,
is taigh air thaigh 'ga reubadh
am broinn a chéile am brùchdadh toit' a' tuiteam?
Is có an nochd tha'g atach
am Bàs a theachd gu grad 'nan cainntibh uile,
no a' spàirn measg chlach is shailthean
air bhàinidh ag gairm air cobhair, is nach cluinnear?
Có an nochd a phàigheas
sean chis àbhaisteach na fala cumant?

Uair dearg mar lod na h-àraich,
uair bàn mar ghile thràighte an eagail éitigh,
a' dìreadh s uair a' teàrnadh,
a' sineadh le sitheadh àrd s ag call a mheudachd,
a' fannachadh car aitil
s ag at mar anail dhiabhuil air dhéinead,
an t-Olc 'na chridhe a 'na chuisle,

chì mi 'na bhuillean a' sìoladh s a' leum e.
Tha'n dreòs 'na oillt air fàire,
'na fhàinne ròis is òir am bun nan speuran,
a' breugnachadh s ag àicheadh
le 'shoillse sèimhe àrsaidh àrd nan reultan.

Bizerta

from the Gaelic of George Campbell Hay
(*Scots version by Hugh MacDiarmid*)

While I'm standin' guard the nicht I see
Awa' doon yonder on the laich skyline
A restless lowe, beatin' its wings
    and scatterin' and dimmin'
A' the starns abune wi'-in reach o' its shine.

You'd think, tho' it's hine awa', there 'ud be heard
Wailin' and lamentation pourin' oot frae't,
That roarin' and screamin', and the yowlin' o' mad dogs,
    'Ud come frae that amber furnace
    a' the noises o' fear and hate,
And flood the haill lift—insteed o'
    which the foul glare
Juist rises and fa's alang the horizon
    in ghastly silence there.

What are the names the nicht o' thae puir streets
Whaur ilka lozen belches flame and
    soot and the screams o' the folk
As hoose eftir hoose is rent and caves
    in in a blash o' smoke?

And whase are the voices cryin' on
    Daith the nicht
In sae mony different tongues to come
    quick and end their plight

79

Or screamin' in frenzy for help and
  no' heard, hid
Under yon muckle heaps a' burnin'
  stanes and beams,
And payin' there the auld accustomed
  tax o' common bluid?

Noo reid like a battlefield puddle, noo wan
Like the dirty pallor o' fear, shootin' up and syne
Sinkin' again, I see Evil like a hammerin'
  pulse or the spasms
O' a hert in the deidthraw aye rax up and dwine
The fitfu' fire, a horror on the horizon, a ring
O' rose and gowd at the fit o' the lift
  belies and denies
The ancient hie beauty and peace o'
  the starns themselves
As its foul glare crines and swells.

An Sealgair Agus An Aois

Cuing mo dhroma an aois a nis,
  rib mo choise, robach, liath:
fear thig eadar soills' is sùilean,
  fear thig eadar rùn is gnìomh.

Fàgaidh e am faillean crotach,
  ris gach dos 's e chuireas sgian:
is, och, b'e 'm bàrr air gach miosguinn
  tighinn eadar mi's an sliabh.

Thug e dhìom a' Chruach Chaorainn,
  's an gunna caol, 's an ealchainn shuas:
bhuin e dhiom mo neart, am meàirleach,
  dh'fhàg a mi gun làmh, gun luaths,

Na'n robh aige corp a ghlacainn,
   's na'n tachrainn ris leis fhéin 's a' bheinn,
bhiodh saltairt ann is fraoch 'ga reubadh,
   's fuil air feur mu'n sgaradh sinn.

The Auld Hunter

from the Gaelic of George Campbell Hay
(Scots version by Hugh MacDiarmid)

Eild comes owre me like a yoke on my craig,
A girn roon' my feet, the lourd and the chill.
Betwixt my sicht and the licht it comes,
It comes betwixt the deed and the will.

This is the thing that warps the sapling
And sets its knife to the aipple's root,
But the warst deed o' a' its spite has been
To filch the hill frae under my foot.

My narrow gun and the paths o' the cruach
Eild has stown, wha's deef and heeds nae grief;
My hand and my foot, this Blear-eyed's stown them
And a' my cheer, like a hertless thief.

But gin Eild were a man that hauns could grapple
And I could come on him secretly
Up there on the hill when naebody passes
Certes! Grass 'ud be trampled or he gat free!

Still Gyte, Man?

'Still gyte, man? Stude I in yere claes
I'd thole nae beggar's nichts an' days,
chap-chappan, whidderan lik a moose,
at ae same cauld an' steekit hoose?'

'What stane has she tae draw yere een?
What gars ye, syne she aye has been
as toom an' hertless as a hoor,
gang sornan kindness at her dure?'

*'Though ye should talk a hunner year,
the windblawn wave will seek the shore,
the muirlan watter seek the sea.
Then, wheesht man. Sae it is wi me.'*

The Old Fisherman

Greet the bights that gave me shelter,
they will hide me no more with the horns of their forelands.
I peer in a haze, my back is stooping;
my dancing days for fishing are over.

The shoot that was straight in the wood withers,
the bracken shrinks red in the rain and shrivels,
the eyes that would gaze in the sun waver;
my dancing days for fishing are over.

The old boat must seek the shingle,
her wasting side hollow the gravel,
the hand that shakes must leave the tiller;
my dancing days for fishing are over.

The sea was good night and morning,
the winds were friends, the calm was kindly—
the snow seeks the burn, the brown fronds scatter;
my dancing days for fishing are over.

ROBERT GARIOCH

Ghaisties

Cauld are the ghaisties in yon kirkyaird
   and cauld the airms
that they mell wi the mists of the timm
    breists of their loves;
at the heid of their bed cauld angels staund on guaird,
   and marble doves.
They ken na the fear of Gode, as they sleep ayont sin,
   nor the terror of man
and there's nane but the angels to glunch
    at their trueloves' chairms,
yet they lang for the reek of the
    creeshy swat frae the skin,
   and the grup of a haund.
But we in the warld are alowe
wi the glawmer of bluid-reid flame
that loups ti the bluid in your tongue's tip
    as it tingles on mine,
   and the howe
o' the back we loo wi oor finger-tips, and the wame,
brent-white, wi' a flush aneath
    like a cramosie wine,
hoo it curves ti meet ma ain!
   O ma sonsie frow
what though the flesh be bruckle,
    and fiends be slee,
the joys of the solid earth we'll pree or they dwine,
we'll lauch at daith, and man, and the fiend, aa three,
    afore we dee.

Sisyphus

Bumpity doun in the corrie gaed whuddran the pitiless whun stane.
Sisyphus, pechan and sweitan, disjaskit, forfeuchan and broun'd-aff,
sat on the heather a hanlawhile, houpan the Boss didna spy him,
seean the terms of his contract includit nae mention of tea-breaks,
syne at the muckle big scunnersom boulder he trauchlit aince mair.
Ach! hou kenspeckle it was, that he ken'd ilka spreckle and blotch
    on't.
Heavan awa at its wecht, he manhaunnlit the bruitt up the brae-
    face,
takkan the easiest gait he had fand in a fudder of dour years,
haudan awa frae the craigs had affrichtit him maist in his youth-
    heid,
feelan his years aa the same, he gaed cannily, tenty of slipped discs.
Eftir an hour and a quarter he warslit his wey to the brae's heid,
hystit his boulder richt up on the tap of the cairn–and it stude
    there!
streikit his length on the chuckie-stanes, houpan the Boss wadna
    spy him,
had a wee look at the scenery, feenisht a pie and a cheese-piece.
Whit was he thinkan about, that he jist gied the boulder a wee
    shove?
Bumpity doun in the corrie gaed whuddran the pitiless whun stane,
Sisyphus dodderan eftir it, shair of his cheque at the month's end.

Elegy

(Edinburgh Sonnet 16)

They are lang deid, folk that I used to ken,
their firm-set lips aa mowdert and agley,
sherp-tempert een rusty amang the cley:
they are baith deid, thae wycelike, bienlie men,

heidmaisters, that had been in pouer for ten
or twenty year afore fate's taiglit wey
brocht me, a young, weill-harnit, blate and fey
new-cleckit dominie, intill their den.

Ane tellt me it was time I learnt to write—
round-haund, he meant—and saw about my hair:
I mind of him, beld-heidit, wi a kyte.

Ane sneerit quarterly—I cuidna square
my savings-bank—and sniftert in his spite.
Weill, gin they arena deid, it's time they were.

GEORGE BRUCE

Inheritance

This which I write now
Was written years ago
Before my birth
In the features of my father.

It was stamped
In the rock formations
West of my hometown.
Not I write,

But, perhaps, William Bruce,
Cooper,
Perhaps here his hand
Well articled in his trade.

Then though my words
Hit out
An ebullition from
City or flower,

There not my faith,
These the paint
Smeared upon
The inarticulate,

The salt-crusted sea-boot,
The red-eyed mackerel,
The plate shining with herring,
And many men,

Seamen and craftsmen and curers,
And behind them
The protest of hundreds of years,
The sea obstinate against the land.

Kinnaird Head

I go North to cold, to home, to Kinnaird,
Fit monument for our time.
This is the outermost edge of Buchan.
Inland the sea birds range,
The tree's leaf has salt upon it,
The tree turns to the low stone wall.
And here a promontory rises towards Norway,
Irregular to the top of thin grey grass
Where the spindrift in storm lays its beads.
The water plugs in the cliff sides,
The gull cries from the clouds
This is the consummation of the plain.

O impregnable and very ancient rock,
Rejecting the violence of water,
Ignoring its accumulations and strategy,
You yield to history nothing.

The Fisherman

As he comes from one of those small houses
Set within the curve of the low cliff
For a moment he pauses
Foot on step at the low lintel
Before fronting wind and sun.
He carries out from within something of the dark
Concealed by heavy curtain,
Or held within the ship under hatches.

Yet with what assurance
The compact body moves,
Head pressed to wind,
His being at an angle
As to anticipate the lurch of earth.

Who is he to contain night
And still walk stubborn
Holding the ground with light feet
And with a careless gait?

Perhaps a cataract of light floods,
Perhaps the apostolic flame.
Whatever it may be
The road takes him from us.
Now the pier is his, now the tide.

Tom Alone on the Beach

With bent back, world's curve on it
I brood over my pretty pool
And hunt the pale, flat, sand-coloured
Fish, with cupped hands, in the cold.

Ah, but my warm heart, with hope
Wrapped in it in the bright afternoon
Feet glittering in the sand,
Eyes on my pale prey, was sure.

Suns have passed, suns have passed,
Skies purple now above the thin sand.
With bent back brooding on the round
World, over my shoulder

I feel the touch of future
In the cold. The little fish
Come not near me, cleaving
To their element and flattening on the sand.

How many years since with sure heart
And prophecy of success
Warmed in it
Did I look with delight on the little fish,

Start with happiness, the warm sun on me?
Now the waters spread horizonwards,
Great skies meet them,
I brood upon incompleted tasks.

A Gateway to the Sea

i. *Corraith, built 1871, Innellan*

This was his dream. To anchor in Time
Where the fierce salt was softened by the rose.
Spindly wrought gates would welcome the wide sea,
Peace would sail into his Victorian calm,
Befriend his pale city children.
All was as he imagined.
The waters brimmed beyond the gates,
A mild surf beckoned the lilies,

The croquet lawn whispered its conversation
To the waters. The yucca prospered
In the Scottish air. This sleight of hand
That conjured four white horses,
Landau, paddle boat and the band,
Waltz and polka and the parasols
On the lawn, could it sustain
The tea-rose and the hushed waters,
Convert the embattled submariners,
Cuttlefish and crab and the sub-lit world?

Evening chimed from the mantelshelf,
The whorled shells gathered the echoes,
Roses spread upon the water,
Serenely gazed from the waters,
The faces of children looked at themselves,
Sails reached up from sails,
Church and house, pier and paddle steamer
Lay tenderly there. Would this pass
With the proper way of taking tea,
With the knowledge of the right answers,
With the words not to be spoken,
And History prevail,
The jungle ocean ravage garden
And house, clad hill
And the parasols, the stock brokers
And the tea-merchants to leave
But a stone, a stone to say
Yes to Time?
In our day
We visited the place. It stood
With the slight green gates
At this end-of-the-world moment,
And not a parasol, not a polka.
And the whorled shells gathered
The evening light and the sea sound
To themselves in air like silk.
Was this moment another dream?

Through the glass's healing eye
Each and every to his kind,
The mauve-grey turtle heaving by
Each and every as his mind.
The star-fish to his rock,
Common crab with his rock face,
Staring cod and Peter's haddock,
Each to his appointed place
Classical leviathan here contained;
All signatories to the pact—
Content to be sustained
By a single mental act.

ii. *The West Port, St Andrews*

Pause stranger at the porch: nothing beyond
This framing arch of stone, but scattered rocks
And sea and these on the low beach
Original to the cataclysm and the dark.

Once one man bent to the stone, another
Dropped the measuring line, a third and fourth
Together lifted and positioned the dressed stone
Making wall and arch; yet others
Settled the iron doors on squawking hinge
To shut without the querulous seas and men.
Order and virtue and love (they say)
Dwelt in the town—but that was long ago.
Then the stranger at the gates, the merchants,
Missioners, the blind beggar with the dog,
The miscellaneous vendors (duly inspected)
Were welcome within the wall that held from sight
The water's brawl. All that was long ago.
Now the iron doors are down to dust,
But the stumps of hinge remain. The arch

Opens to the element—the stones dented
And stained to green and purple and rust.
Pigeons settle on the top. Stranger,
On this winter afternoon pause at the porch,
For the dark land beyond stretches
To the unapproachable element, bright
As night falls and with the allurement of peace,
Concealing under the bland feature, possession.
Not all the agitations of the world
Articulate the ultimate question as do those waters
Confining the memorable and the forgotten;
Relics, records, furtive occasions—Caesar's politics
And he who was drunk last night:
Rings, diamants, snuff boxes, warships.
Also the less worthy garments of worthy men.

Prefer then this handled stone, now ruined
While the sea mists wind about the arch.
The afternoon dwindles, night concludes,
The stone is damp, unyielding to the touch
But crumbling in the strain and stress
Of the years: the years winding about the arch,
Settling in the holes and crevices, moulding
The dressed stone. Once, one man bent to it,
Another dropped the measuring line, a third
And fourth positioned to make wall and arch
Theirs. Pause, stranger, at this small town's edge—
The European sun knew those streets
O Jesu parvule, Christus Victus, Christus Victor,
The bells singing from their towers, the waters
Whispering to the waters, the air tolling
To the air—the faith, the faith, the faith.

All this was long ago. The lights
Are out, the town is sunk in sleep,
The boats are rocking at the pier,
The vague winds beat about the streets—
Choir and altar and chancel are gone.

Under the touch the guardian stone remains.
Holding memory, reproving desire, securing hope
In the stop of water, in the lull of night
Before dawn kindles a new day.

SORLEY MACLEAN

Dain Do Eimhir Liv

Bu tu camhanaich air a' Chuilthionn
's latha suilbhir air a' Chlàraich
grian air a h-uilinn anns an òr-shruth
agus ròs geal bristeadh fàire.

Lainnir sheòl air linne ghrianaich,
gorm a' chuain is iarmailt àr-bhuidh,
an òg-mhaduinn 'na do chuailean
's 'na do ghruaidhean soilleir àlainn.

Mo leug camhanaich is oidhche
t' aodann 's do choibhneas gràdhach,
ged tha bior glas an dòlais
troimh chliabh m' òg-mhaidne sàthte.

Ye Were the Dawn

from the Gaelic of Sorley Maclean
(*Scots version by Douglas Young*)

Ye were the dawn on the hills o the Cuillin,
the bousum day on the Clarach arisan,
the sun on his elbucks i the gowden flume,
the whyte rose-fleur that braks the horizon.

Gesserant sails on a skinklan frith,
gowd-yalla lyft and blue o the sea . . .
the fresh mornin in your heid o hair
and your clear face wi its bonnie blee.

Gowdie, my gowdie o dawn and the derk
your loesome gentrice, your brou sae rare . . .
albeid wi the dullyart stang o dule
the breist o youth's been thirlit sair.

Calbharaigh

Cha n-eil mo shùil air Calbharaigh
no air Bethlehem an àigh
ach air cùil ghrod an Glaschu
far bheil an lobhadh fàis
agus air seòmar an Dun-éideann,
seòmar bochdainn 's cràidh
far am bheil an naoidhean creuchdach
ri aonagraich gu bhàs.

My Een are Nae on Calvary

from the Gaelic of Sorley Maclean
  (*Scots version by Douglas Young*)

My een are nae on Calvary
or the Bethlehem they praise,
but on shitten back-lands in Glesca toun
whaur growan life decays,
and a stairheid room in an Embro land,
a chalmer o puirtith and skaith,
whaur monie a shilpet bairnikie
gaes smoorit doun til daith.

Ban-Ghaidheal

Am faca Tu i, Iùdhaich mhóir,
ri an abrar Aon Mhac Dhe?
Am fac' thu a coltas air Do thriall
ri strì an fhìon-lios chéin?

An cuallach mheasan air a druim,
fallus searbh air mala is gruaidh;
's a' mhìos chreadha trom air cùl
a cinn chrùibte, bhochd, thruaigh.

Chanfhaca Tu i, Mhic an t-saoir,
ri an abrar Rìgh na Glòir,
am measg nan cladach carrach, siar,
fo fhallus cliabh a lòin.

An t-earrach so agus so chaidh
's gach fichead earrach bho an tùs
tharruing ise an fheamainn fhuar
chum biadh a cloinn is duais an tùir.

Is gach fichead foghar tha air triall
chaill i samhradh buidh nam blàth;
is threabh an dubh chosnadh an clais
tarsuinn mìnead ghil a clàir.

Agus labhair T'eaglais chaomh
mu staid chaillte a h-anama thruaigh;
agus leag an cosnadh dian
a corp gu sàmhchair dhuibh an uaigh.

Is thriall a tìm mar shnighe dubh
a' drùdhadh tughaidh fàrdaich bochd;
mheal ise an dubh chosnadh cruaidh;
is glas a cadal suain an nochd.

Hielant Woman

from the Gaelic of Sorley Maclean
(*Scots version by Douglas Young*)

Hae ye seen her, ye unco Jew,
ye that they caa Ae Son o God?
Thon trauchlit woman i the far vine-yaird,
saw ye the likes o her on your road?

A creelfu o corn upo her spaul,
swyte on her brou, saut swyte on her cheek,
a yirthen pat on the tap o her heid,
her laigh-bouit heid, dwaiblie and sick.

Ye haena seen her, ye son o the vricht,
wi 'King o Glory' fowk roose ye weel,
on the staney westland machars thonder
swytan under her wechtit creel.

This spring o the year is by and gane
and twenty springs afore it spent,
sin she's hikeit creels o cauld wrack
for her bairns' meat and the laird's rent.

Twenty hairsts hae dwineit awa,
she's tint her simmer's gowden grace,
while the sair trauchle o the black wark
pleud its rigg on her clear face.

Her puir saul is eternallie tint,
as threeps aye your kindly Kirk;
and endless wark has brocht her corp
to the graff's peace, lown and derk.

Her time gaed by like black sleek
through an auld thaikit hous-rig seepan;
she bruikit aye sair black wark,
and gray the nicht is her lang sleepin

An Trom-Laighe

Oidhche de'n dà bhliadhna
'N uair shaoil mi gun do chreuchdadh
Mo luaidh le giamh cho miosa
'S a bh'air mnaoi bho linn Eubha,
Bha sinn comhla am bruadar
Ri taobh a' bhalla chloiche
Tha eadar cluich ghart ghillean
Is nighean mo cheud sgoile,
Bha i eadar mo lamhan
'S mo bheul a' dol g'a bilibh
'N uair straon an ceann oillteil
Bho chùl a' bhalla 'n clisgeadh,
Is rinn na cràgan ciara
Fada bréine mo sgornan
A ghlacadh an greim obann
'S lean briathran an eu-dòchais:
'Tha thu ghloic air dheireadh.'

The Widdreme

from the Gaelic of Sorley Maclean
(*Scots version by Sydney Goodsir Smith*)

Ae nicht o thae twa year
Whan I thocht ma luve
Was strak wi a skaith as dure
As wumman's had sen Eve,
We were thegither in a dwaum
By the stane dyke that staunds
Atween the loons' and lassies' yairds
O ma first schuil.
                    Ma airms
Were round her and ma lips
Seekan her mou
Whan the laithlie gorgon's heid stuid up

96

On a sudden frae hint the waa,
And the lang mirk ugsome fingers graipt
Ma craig wi a sudden grup—
And then the words o weirdless dule:
'Owre blate, ye fuil!'

DOUGLAS YOUNG

Sabbath i the Mearns

The geans are fleuran whyte i the green Howe o the Mearns;
wastlan winds are blawan owre the Mownth's cauld glacks,
whaur the whaups wheep round their nesties among the fog and
    ferns;
and the ferm-touns stand gray and lown, ilk wi its yalla stacks.
The kirk is skailan, and the fowk in Sabbath stand o blacks
are doucely haudan hame til their denners wi the bairns,
the young anes daffan and auld neebours haean cracks.

Thon's bien and canty livin for auld-farrant fermer-fowk
wha wark their lives out on the land, the bonnie Laigh o Mearns.
They pleu and harra, saw and reap, clatt neeps and tattie-howk,
and dinna muckle fash theirsels wi ither fowk's concerns.
There's whiles a chyld that's unco wild, but sune the wildest learns
gin ye're nae a mensefu fermer-chiel ye's be naething but a gowk,
and the auld weys are siccar, auld and siccar like the sterns.

They werena aye like thon, this auld Albannach race,
whas stanes stand heich upo' the Mownth whaur the wild whaup
    caas.
Focht for libertie wi Wallace, luikit tyrants i the face,
stuid a siege wi leal Ogilvie for Scotland's king and laws,[1]
i the Whigs' Vaut o Dunnottar testified for Freedom's cause.
Is there onie Hope to equal the Memories o this place?
The last Yerl Marischal's deid, faan doun his castle waas.

[1] Sir George Ogilvie of Barras held Dunnottar Castle, with Charles II's
regalia inside, against the Cromwellian General Monk.

For a Wife in Jizzen

Lassie, can ye say
 whaur ye hae been,
whaur ye ha come frae,
 whatna ferlies seen?

Eftir the bluid and swyte,
 the warsslin o yestreen,
ye ligg forfochten, whyte,
 prouder nor any queen.

Albeid ye hardly see me
 I read it in your een,
sae saft blue and dreamy,
 mindan whaur ye've been.

Anerly wives ken
 the ruits o joy and tene,
  the march o daith and birth,
   the tryst o luve and strife
i the howdumbdeidsunsheen,
 fire, air, water, yirth
  mellan to mak new life,
lauchan and greetan, feiman and serene.

Dern frae aa men
 the ferlies ye ha seen.

For the Old Highlands

That old lonely lovely way of living
in Highland places,—twenty years a-growing,
twenty years flowering, twenty years declining—
father to son, mother to daughter giving
ripe tradition; peaceful bounty flowing;

one harmony all tones of life combining—
old, wise ways, passed like the dust blowing.

That harmony of folk and land is shattered,—
the yearly rhythm of things, the social graces,
peat-fire and music, candle-light and kindness.
Now they are gone it seems they never mattered,
much, to the world, those proud and violent races,
clansmen and chiefs whose passioned greed and blindness
made desolate these lovely lonely places.

Fife Equinox

Ae day and ae nicht a yowden-druft
fae the cauld nor-aist has whusslit and pufft
and blawn the craws about the luft,
blatteran sairlie;
it reeshlit the wuids and gart them shuft
like a breer o barley.

The cypress-busses are aa blawn cruikit,
the greens are as clorty as onie doocot;
the wind-faan epples'll hae to be cuikit
afore they get waur.
The plooms are aa wersh, they're that sair droukit
and clortit wi glaur.

The Shepherd's Dochter

Lay her and lea her here i the gantan grund,
the blythest, bonniest lass o the countryside,
crined in a timber sark, hapt wi the pride
o hothous flouers, the dearest that could be fund.

Her faither and brithers stand, as suddentlie stunned
   wi the wecht o dule; douce; douce neebours side by side
   wreist and fidge, sclent-luikan, sweirt tae bide
while the Minister's duin and his threep gane wir the wind.

The murners skail, thankfu tae lea thon place
   whar the blythest, bonniest lass liggs in the mouls,
     Lent lilies lowp and cypresses stand stieve,
   Time tae gae back tae the darg, machines and tools
     and beasts and seeds, the things men uis tae live,
and lea the puir lass there in her state o Grace.

Last Lauch

The Minister said it wald dee,
   the cypress buss I plantit.
But the buss grew til a tree,
   naething dauntit.

It's growan, stark and heich,
   derk and straucht and sinister,
kirkyairdie-like and dreich.
   But whaur's the Minister?

J. F. HENDRY

Inverbeg

Sliced with shade and scarred with snow
A mountain breaks like Mosaic rock
And through the lilt of mist there flow
Restless rivers of pebble, pocked
And speckled, where moss and the centuries grow.

Tree, married to cloud as stem is to feather,
Branches and straddles the convex of sky.
Death is aflame in the bracken where heather
Rears semaphore smoke into high
Blue messenger fire through soundless weather.

Below, like bees, the ivies swarm,
Cast in leaping veins, their trunk, a crippled
Animal of thighs pounced from loch-water, storms
The slated shores of the past into ripples
Interpreting man's fretted cuneiform.

Tir-nan-Og

A man is born, a man dies,
And in between are miseries.

In between he is alive
But cannot be allowed to live

Since, body's hunger never fed,
The mind is never satisfied

And hands and feet and head and eyes
Are hourly humbled to the knees.

A man dies, a man is born,
And in between a burden borne.

In between, by force of love,
A grief in life is made alive

Whose mind is more than satisfied
And body's hunger always fed,

Whose hands rise up from feet and knees,
Encircle head and rub the eyes.

The Ship

Here is a ship you made
Out of my breasts and sides
As I lay dead in the yards
Under the hammers.

Here is the hull you built
Out of a heart of salt,
Sky-rent, the prey of birds
Strung on the longshore.

Here is her rigging bound
Nerve, sinew, ice and wind
Blowing through the night
The starred dew of beads.

Here her ribs of silver
Once steerless in a culvert
Climb the laddered centuries
To hide a cloud in a frame.

The Constant North

(For Dee)

Encompass me, my lover,
With your eyes' wide calm.
Though noonday shadows are assembling doom,
The sun remains when I remember them;
And death, if it should come,
Must fall like quiet snow from such clear skies.

Minutes we snatched from the unkind winds
Are grown into daffodils by the sea's
Edge, mocking its green miseries;

Yet I seek you hourly still, over
A new Atlantis loneliness, blind
As a restless needle held by the constant north we always have in
  mind.

W. S. GRAHAM

Many Without Elegy

Many without elegy interpret a famous heart
Held with a searoped saviour to direct
The land. This morning moves aside
Sucking disaster and my bread
On the hooped fields of Eden's mountain
Over the crews of wrecked seagrain.

There they employ me. I rise to the weed that harps
More shipmark to capsizing, more to lament
Under the whitewashed quenched skerries
The washed-away dead. Hullo you mercies
Morning drowns tail and all and bells
Bubble up rigging as the saint falls.

Many dig deeper in joy and are shored with
A profit clasped in a furious swan-necked prow
To sail against spout of this monumental loss
That jibles with no great nobility its cause.
That I can gather, this parched offering
Of a dry hut out of wrong weeping.

Saying 'there's my bleached-in-tears opponent
Prone on his brothering bolster in the week
Of love for unbandaged unprayed for men.'
Gone to no end but each man's own.
So far they are, creation's whole memory
Now never fears their death or day.

Many out of the shades project a heart
Famous for love and only what they are
To each self's landmark marked among
The dumb scenery of weeping.
I come in sight and duty of these
For food and fuel of a talking blaze.

Here as the morning moved my eyes achieve
Further through elegy. There is the dolphin
Reined with searopes stitching a heart
To swim through blight. No, I'll inherit
No keening in my mountain head or sea
Nor fret for few who die before I do.

O Gentle Queen

O gentle queen of the afternoon
Wave the last orient of tears.
No daylight comet ever breaks
On so sweet an archipelago
As love on love.

The fundamental negress built
In a cloudy descant of the stars
Surveys no sorrow, invents no limits
Till laughter the watcher of accident
Sways off to God.

O gentle queen of the afternoon
The dawn is rescued dead and risen.
Promise, O bush of blushing joy,
No daylight comet ever breaks
On so sweet an archipelago
As love on love.

At That Bright Cry Set on the Heart's Headwaters

At that bright cry set on the heart's head waters
I'm handed keys. I'm drifted well away.
Ahoy, shall I shout, emigrant to save me?
A packet of Irish returning to hoist the wars
Rendering wherein the white world they trod.
Beside to sea I'm kindled by its garments.

At that cupped cry my kelp puffs up its hints,
Was mortal-caulked before it fell to the arrived
Contraries and kegs, bedlams of victorious vale.
And was before it fell to this formal ash
The manned quarters of my imagination's courage.
Bedside to earth and something of a man, I say
And hoist to words this arrival, and see sail
The deadly manroped hearties of a holy sea-vessel.

Letter II

Burned in this element
To the bare bone, I am
Trusted on the language.
I am to walk to you
Through the night and through
Each word I burn bright in
On this wide reach. And you,
Within what arms you lie,
Hear my burning ways
Across these darknesses
That move and merge like foam.
Lie in the world's room,
My dear, and contribute
Here where all dialogues write.

Younger in the towered
Tenement of night he heard
The shipyards with nightshifts
Of lathes turning their shafts.
His voice was a humbled ear
Hardly turned to her.
Then in a welding flash
He found his poetry arm
And turned the coat of his trade.
From where I am I hear
Clearly his heart beat over
Clydeside's far hammers
And the nightshipping firth.
What's he to me? Only
Myself I died from into
These present words that move.
In that high tenement
I got a great grave.

Tonight in sadly need
Of you I move inhuman
Across this space of dread
And silence in my mind.
I walk the dead water
Burning language towards
You where you lie in the dark
Ascension of all words.
Yet where? Where do you lie
Lost to my cry and hidden
Away from the word's downfall?
O offer some way tonight
To make your love take place
In every word. Reply.
Time's branches burn to hear.
Take heed. Reply. Here
I am driven burning on
This loneliest element. Break
Break me out of this night,

This silence where you are not,
Nor any whithin earshot.
Break break me from this high
Helmet of idiocy.

Water water wallflower
Growing up so high
We are all children
We all must die.
Except Willie Graham
The fairest of them all.
He can dance and he can sing
And he can turn his face to the wall.
Fie, fie, fie for shame
Turn your face to the wall again.

Yes laugh then cloudily laugh
Though he sat there as deaf
And worn to a stop
As the word had given him up.
Stay still. That was the sounding
Sea he moved on burning
His still unending cry.
That night hammered and waved
Its starry shipyard arms,
And it came to inherit
His death where these words merge.
This is his night writ large.
In Greenock the bright breath
Of night's array shone forth
On the nightshifting town.
Thus younger burning in
The best of his puny gear
He early set out
To write him to this death
And to that great breath
Taking of the sea,
The graith of Poetry.

My musing love lie down
Within his arms. He dies
Word by each word into

Myself now at this last
Word I die in. This last.

From *The Night Fishing*

Very gently struck
The quay night bell.

Now within the dead
Of night and the dead
Of my life I hear
My name called from far out.
I'm come to this place
(Come to this place)
Which I'll not pass
Though one shall pass
Wearing seemingly
This look I move as.
This staring second
Breaks my home away
Through always every
Night through every whisper
From the first that once
Named me to the bone.
Yet this place finds me
And forms itself again.
This present place found me.
Owls from on the land.
Gulls cry from the water.
And that wind honing
The roof-ridge is out of

Nine hours west on the main
Ground with likely a full
Gale unwinding it.

Gently the quay bell
Strikes the held air.

Strikes the held air like
Opening a door
So that all the dead
Brought to harmony
Speak out on silence.

I bent to the lamp. I cupped
My hand to the glass chimney.
Yet it was a stranger's breath
From out of my mouth that
Shed the light. I turned out
Into the salt dark
And turned my collar up.

And now again almost
Blindfold with the bright
Hemisphere unprised
Ancient overhead,
I am befriended by
This sea which utters me.
The hull slewed out through
The lucky turn and trembled
Under way then. The twin
Screws spun sweetly alive
Spinning position away.

Far out faintly calls
The continual sea.

Now within the dead
Of night and the dead

Of all my life I go.
I'm one ahead of them
Turned in below.
I'm borne, in their eyes,
Through the staring world.

The present opens its arms.

ADAM DRINAN

Successful Scot

Gold pins and pearls of Columba,
   how gross they grow by your drive,
studding an English summer
   with the back-end of your life,
     beknighted and pompous Scot!

By adding figure to figure
   you have developed never,
you have just grown bigger and bigger
   like this wee wort from the heather;
     and size is all you have got.

Your mind set toward London,
   your belly pushing to success,
from the very day that you won
   the Bursary of the West,
     have flagged and faltered not.

Not much has your face altered!
   The man has the mouth of the child.
The Position you planted and watered
   expands from the lad's desires
     as if bound in a pot.

And would you return (for the fishing)
    to your island of humbler hours,
there in your tailored wishes
    you would trample your youth in this flower
        that you have forgotten:

Or spending a stay-at-home summer,
    you will never know what they suffer,
these bloated flowers of Columba;
    you will own the youth of others,
        and never know what.

Love Song

Soft as the wind your hair,
gull-gleaming your breasts.
I hoard no treasures there.
I do not grope for rest.
I seek you as my home,
that all your sensitive life
may fuse into my own,
and the world match with my wife.

I carry you out of this
to no enchanted isle.
Blood is tart in your kiss,
and no dream in your smile.
Bitter, bitter the hours
and coasts of our patrol.
Foggy this Minch of ours.
But I sail with your soul.

I come to you in the flame
of a burst and broken land.
There is acid in my brain
and withering in my hand.

Your touch will plot us wise,
your quiet keep it true;
and joy be the starlight
to what we have to do.

From *The Men on the Rocks*

Our pastures are bitten and bare
our wool is blown to the winds
our mouths are stopped and dumb
our oatfields weaks and thin.
Nobody fishes the loch
nobody stalks the deer.
Let us go down to the sea.
The friendly sea likes to be visited.

Our fathers sleep in the cemetery
their boats, cracked, by their side.
The sea turns round in his sleep
pleasurecraft nod on the tide.
Sea ducks slumber on waves
sea eagles have flown away.
Let us put out to sea.
The fat sea likes to be visited.

Fat sea, what's on your shelf?
all the grey night we wrestled.
To muscle, to skill, to petrol,
Hook oo rin yo! . . . one herring!
and of that only the head.
Dogfishes had the rest,
A parting gift from the sea.
The merry waves like to be visited.

Merry sea, what have you sent us?
A rusty English trawler?

The crew put into the hotel
the engineer overhauls her.
Gulls snatch offal to leeward.
We on the jetty await
gifts of the cod we can't afford.
The free sea likes to be visited.

Free were our father's boats
whose guts were strown on the shore.
Steam ships were bought by the rich
cheap from the last war.
They tear our nets to pieces
and the sea gives them our fishes.
Even he favours the rich.
The false sea likes to be visited.

From *The Ghosts of the Strath*

Long blue shadow of salmon lying,
    shot shell of leaping silver,
using the lull and the flies
    to practise for the rough river,
stay down on the salt sea stones,
    learn there, you yet-free fishes.
Your sweet hope to come home
    was once on the hillside fishers.

Salmon may leap falls;
    we deeps of the linn may master:
but weeds grow up our walls,
    hearts whip in airy water.
Up in the rich meads
    such the rich men's power is,
Only wrens are safe in streams
    and sheep in houses.

The great power had its magic!
  with strong spells of paper
money and law raised lairds;
  burnt crops bewitched labour.
No cunning of fish-lore
  will conjure our safe return;
but the same black arts be ours—
  from the need to burn, to the burning.

Measures

Three measures of breadth I take
that the heart, the hand, and the foot make:
  the candid inches between the eyes of confidence,
  the width of a gull's back in the hand that shot it,
  and the stretch of a water that cannot be walked upon.

And three measures of slenderness I put to these,
in which the eye, the ear, and the mind meet:
  the slimness of a boy's ankle while he is alive to dance,
  the whisper that draws a hill across a strath,
  and that which separates self-respect from self-regard.

G. S. FRASER

Meditation of a Patriot

The posters show my country blonde and green,
Like some sweet siren, but the travellers know
How dull the shale sky is, the airs how keen,
And how our boorish manners freeze like snow.
Romantic Scotland was an emigrant,
Half-blooded, and escaped from sullen weather.
Here, we toss off a dram to drown a cough

And whisky has the trade-mark of the heather.
My heart yearns southwards as the shadows slant,
I wish I were an exile and I rave:
　　With Byron and with Lermontov
　　Romantic Scotland's in the grave.

In Glasgow, that damned sprawling evil town,
I interview a vulgar editor,
Who, brawny, self-made, looks me up and down
And seems to wonder what my sort is for.
Do I write verse? Ah, man, but that is bad . . .
And, too polite, I fawn upon this tough,
But when I leave him, O my heart is sad.
He sings alone who in this province sings.
I kick a lamp-post, and in drink I rave:
　　With Byron and with Lermontov
　　Romantic Scotland's in the grave.

In the far islands to the north and west
Mackenzie and MacDiarmid have their peace.
St. Andrews soothes that critic at her breast
Whose polished verse ne'er gave his soul release.
I have no islands and no ancient stone,
Only the sugary granite glittering crisp
Pleases the eye, but turns affection off,
Hard rhetoric, that never learned to lisp.
This town has beauty, but I walk alone
And to the flat and sallow sands I rave:
　　With Byron and with Lermontov
　　Romantic Scotland's in the grave.

To Hugh MacDiarmid

Since mine was never the heroic gesture,
　　Trained to slick city from my childhood's days,
Only a rambling garden's artful leisure
　　Giving my mind its privacy and ease.

Since Poverty for me has never sharpened
   Her single tooth, and since Adversity
So far has failed to jab me with her hair-pin,
   I marvel who my Scottish Muse can be.

I am Convention's child, the cub reporter,
   The sleek, the smooth, conservatively poised:
Abandoned long ago by Beauty's daughter;
   Tamed like a broncho, and commercialised!

Perhaps I have a heart that feels. . . . I wonder!
   At least I can salute your courage high,
Your thought that burns language to a cinder,
   Your anger, and your angry poet's joy.

O warrior, with the world and wind against you,
   Old sea-bird, in your bleak and rocky coign,
Only my fears can follow where you fly to . . .
   Beneath these rocks, how many souls lie slain!

Your journey has not been the private journey
   Through a mad loveliness, of Hölderlin.
Against the windmills, sir, you chose to tourney.
   And yet, by marvellous chance, you hold your own.

O true bright sword! Perhaps, like Mithridates,
   Before the night has fallen, you may say:
'Now I am satisfied: at least my hate is:
   Now let me die: I saw the English flee.'

Facing boys' faces, whom your world of thunder
   Is massing clouds for, whom the violet forks
Seek out from heaven . . . simulating candour
   I face both ways! A secret question carks.

Because my love was never for the common
   But only for the rare, the singular air,
Or the undifferenced and naked human,
   Your Keltic mythos shudders me with fear.

What a race has is always crude and common,
    And not the human or the personal:
I would take sword up only for the human,
    Not to revive the broken ghosts of Gael.

Lean Street

Here, where the baby paddles in the gutter,
    Here, in the slaty greyness and the gas,
Here, where the women wear dark shawls and mutter
    A hasty word as other women pass.

Telling the secret, telling, clucking and tutting,
    Sighing, or saying that it served her right,
The bitch!—the words and weather both are cutting
    In Causewayend, on this November night.

At pavement's end and in the slaty weather
    I stare with glazing eyes at meagre stone,
Rain and the gas are sputtering together
    A dreary tune! O leave my heart alone,

O leave my heart alone, I tell my sorrows,
    For I will soothe you in a softer bed
And I will numb your grief with fat tomorrows
    Who break your milk teeth on this stony bread!

They do not hear. Thought stings me like an adder,
    A doorway's sagging plumb-line squints at me,
The fat sky gurgles like a swollen bladder
    With the foul rain that rains on poverty.

Hometown Elegy

(for Aberdeen in Spring)

Glitter of mica at the windy corners,
Tar in the nostrils, under blue lamps budding
Like bubbles of glass and blue buds of a tree,
Night-shining shopfronts, or the sleek sun flooding
The broad abundant dying sprawl of the Dee:
For these and for their like my thoughts are mourners
That yet shall stand, though I come home no more,
Gas works, white ballroom, and the red brick baths
And salmon nets along a mile of shore,
Or beyond the municipal golf-course, the moorland paths
And the country lying quiet and full of farms.
This is the shape of a land that outlasts a strategy
And is not to be taken with rhetoric or arms.
Or my own room, with a dozen books on the bed
(Too late, still musing what I mused, I lie
And read too lovingly what I have read),
Brantome, Spinoza, Yeats, the bawdy and wise,
Continuing their interminable debate,
With no conclusion, they conclude too late,
When their wisdom has fallen like a grey pall on my eyes.
Syne we maun part, there sall be nane remeid—
Unless my country is my pride, indeed,
Or I can make my town that homely fame
That Byron has, from boys in Carden Place,
Struggling home with books to midday dinner,
For whom he is not the romantic sinner,
The careless writer, the tormented face,
The hectoring bully or the noble fool,
But, just like Gordon or like Keith, a name:
A tall, proud statue at the Grammar School.

The Traveller has Regrets

The traveller has regrets
For the receding shore
That with its many nets
Has caught, not to restore,
The white lights in the bay,
The blue lights on the hill,
Though night with many stars
May travel with him still,
But night has nought to say,
Only a colour and shape
Changing like cloth shaking,
A dancer with a cape
Whose dance is heart-breaking,
Night with its many stars
Can warn travellers
There's only time to kill
And nothing much to say:
But the blue lights on the hill,
The white lights in the bay
Told us the meal was laid
And that the bed was made
And that we could not stay.

ROBERT MACLELLAN

Sang

There's a reid lowe in yer cheek,
Mither, and a licht in yer ee,
And ye sing like the shuilfie in the slae,
But no for me.

The man that cam the day,
Mither, that ye ran to meet,

He drapt his gun and fondlet ye
And I was left to greit.

Ye served him kail frae the pat,
Mither, and meat frae the bane.
Ye brocht him cherries frae the gean,
And I gat haurdly ane.

And nou he lies in yer bed,
Mither, and the licht growes dim,
And the sang ye sing as ye hap me ower
Is meant for him.

Arran

It is an ageless sang this auld isle sings
In the burn born alang the scree fute
By riven craigs whaur the black raven brings
The still-born lamb to its nest by the rowan rute;

In runnels hidden in the corrie heid
To stags in velvet whaur their leader fell,
And hinds heavy wi the fruit o his spent seed
Makin milk and horn for birth and dule;

Syne in the gill whaur the gled breists the spray,
Gleg for the muir-hen skeerie in her nest,
And the yowe cries for her lamb lost amang the grey
Banes o the cairn whaur men were laid to rest

That had danced in the wame o time in rings o stane
To gar the sun turn and the new day daw.
It sings in the muirland linns by a tummlet waa
Whaur ance an abbot brocht a martyr's bane,

And wrote Christ's passion in a book o prayer,
And lit his haly rude, and rang his bell.
Nou in the bents the shepherd warks his pair
And his whistle stirs the whaup, and the hills fill,

And whan the dirl is dune the linns sing still
And the rushes at the tails o the pules sing,
An ourie sang that soochs ower the broken sill
And the hearth-stane smoored in a flair o ling

In a hoose that was haill whan sheep tuimed the clachans.
The wind frae the balloch soochs in the bent ash,
And gulls wail ower carrion in the breckans,
And the lambs o the driven yowes girn and fash.

Doun nou in the dim fernie deeps
O the dank den whaur the braid torrent faas
Ower mossie rocks aneth heich hingin shaws
It sings whaur the ousel dips and the wagtail creeps

And the otter dives and the quick troots scatter;
Syne doun again and oot on the last run
To the holms in the wide dale whaur the watter
Winds saftly by the bien ferm white in the sun

To meet the sea, soondless, at the flood o the tide.
The gulls and waders staun husht for the turn.
It sings sleep to the clachan deid in graves o thorn
By the grey ruin whaur ance their banns were cried.

NORMAN MCCAIG

Wet Snow

White tree on black tree,
Ghostly appearance fastened on another,
Called up by harsh spells of this wintry weather
You stand in the night as though to speak to me.

I could almost
Say what you do not fail to say; that's why
I turn away, in terror, not to see
A tree stand there hugged by its own ghost.

November Night, Edinburgh

The night tinkles like ice in glasses.
Leaves are glued to the pavement with frost.
The brown air fumes at the shop windows,
Tries the doors, and sidles past.

I gulp down winter raw. The heady
Darkness swirls with tenements.
In a brown fuzz of cottonwool
Lamps fade up crags, die into pits.

Frost in my lungs is harsh as leaves
Scraped up on paths. – I look up, there,
A high roof sails, at the mast-head
Fluttering a grey and ragged star.

The world's a bear shrugged in his den.
It's snug and close in the snoring night.
And outside like chrysanthemums
The fog unfolds its bitter scent.

Edinburgh Courtyard in July

Hot light is smeared as thick as paint
On these ramshackle tenements. Stones smell
Of dust. Their hoisting into quaint
Crowsteps, corbels, carved with fool and saint,
Holds fathoms of heat, like water in a well.

Cliff-dwellers have poked out from their
High cave-mouths brilliant rags on drying-lines;
They hang still, dazzling in the glare,
And lead the eye up, ledge by ledge, to where
A chimney's tilted helmet winks and shines.

And water from a broken drain
Splashes a glassy hand out in the air
That breaks in an unbraiding rain
And falls still fraying, to become a stain
That spreads by footsteps, ghosting everywhere.

Boats

The boat need carry no more than a live man
And there's a meaning, a cargo of centuries.
They make a hieroglyph on the sea that can
Cramp circumnavigations in one round gaze.

Hard sailors put out from books and ancient tales.
They have names that chink like gold or clash like ice.
They shred coarse fog or beat suns with their sails,
Pooled in iambics or tossed on hexameters.

Days jagged on skerries, nights signalling with foam
Were golden fleece, white whale, lost Ithaca.
No answering star could call these wanderers home;
Each cape they doubled jutted from history.

Watch this one, ancient Calum. He crabs his boat
Sideways across the tide, every stroke a groan –
Ancient Calum no more, but legends afloat.
No boat ever sailed with a crew of one alone.

Celtic Cross

The implicated generations made
This symbol of their lives, a stone made light
By what is carved on it.
                              The plaiting masks,
But not with involutions of a shade,
What a stone says and what a stone cross asks.

Something that is not mirrored by nor trapped
In webs of water or bag-nets of cloud;
The tangled mesh of weed
                              lets it go by.
Only men's minds could ever have unmapped
Into abstraction such a territory.

No green bay going yellow over sand
Is written on by winds to tell a tale
Of death-dishevelled gull
                              or heron, stiff
As a cruel clerk with gaunt writs in his hand
–Or even of light, that makes its depths a cliff.

Singing responses order otherwise.
The tangled generations ravelled out
In links of song whose sweet
                              strong choruses
Are these stone involutions to the eyes
Given to the ear in abstract vocables.

The stone remains, and the cross, to let us know
Their unjust, hard demands, as symbols do.
But on them twine and grow
                              beneath the dove
Serpents of wisdom whose cool statements show
Such understanding that it seems like love.

Byre

The thatched roof rings like heaven where mice
Squeak small hosannahs all night long,
Scratching its golden pavements, skirting
The gutter's crystal river-song.

Wild kittens in the world below
Glare with one flaming eye through cracks,
Spurt in the straw, are tawny brooches
Splayed on the chests of drunken sacks.

The dimness becomes darkness as
Vast presences come mincing in,
Swagbellied Aphrodites, swinging
A silver slaver from each chin.

And all is milky, secret, female.
Angels are hushed and plain straws shine.
And kittens miaow in circles, stalking
With tail and hindleg one straight line.

Assisi

The dwarf with his hands on backwards
Sat, slumped like a half-filled sack
On tiny twisted legs from which
Sawdust might run,

Outside the three tiers of churches built
In honour of St. Francis, brother
Of the poor, talker with birds, over whom
He had the advantage
Of not being dead yet.

His look owed its slyness
To the fact
That he had no neck.

A priest explained
How clever it was of Giotto
To make his frescoes tell stories
That would reveal to the illiterate the goodness
Of God and the suffering
Of His Son. I understood
The explanation and
The cleverness.

A rush of tourists, clucking contentedly,
Fluttered after him as he scattered
The grain of the Word.
It was they who had passed
The ruined temple outside, whose eyes
Wept pus, whose back was higher
Than his head, whose lopsided mouth
Said *Grazie* in a voice as sweet
As a child's when she speaks to her mother
Or a bird's when it spoke
To St. Francis.

SYDNEY GOODSIR SMITH

Loch Leven

Tell me was a glorie ever seen
As the morn I left ma lass
'Fore licht i the toun o snaw
And saw the daw
O' burnan crammassie
Turn the grey ice
O' Mary's Loch Leven
To sheenan bress—
An kent the glorie and the gleen
Was but the waukenin o her een?

Largo

Ae boat anerlie nou
Fishes frae this shore,
Ae black drifter lane,
Riggs the cramasie daw—
Aince was a fleet, but nou
Ae boat alane gaes out.

War or peace, the trawlers win
And the youth turns awa
Bricht wi baubles nou
And thirled to factory or store;
Their faithers fished their ain,
Unmaistered; ane remains.

And never the clock rins back,
The free days are owre;
The warld shrinks, we luik
Mair t'oor maisters ilka hour—
Whan yon lane boat I see
Daith and rebellion blinn ma ee.

Sahara

Inexorable on ye stride,
Fate, like a desert wind;
Agin your vast unpassioned pride
I pit ma saul and haund,
As the wild Bedouin
Tykes gowl at the mune.

II

March, ye luveless Cailleach, blaw
Til the dumbest, mirkest end,
And whan the yerth's a blastit skau
As toom Sahara brunt and blind
There, daft and damned wi raivan ee,
Adam, greinan tae be free.

Spleen

Steir bogle, sqaut bogle
Bogle o sweirness and stuperie;
Wersh bogle, wae bogle,
Bogle o drumlie apathie;
Thir twa haud this fule in duress—
Malancolie, Idleness.

In duress vile ye muckle fule,
Cock o your midden o sloth and stour,
Geck o the yill and a restless saul
I dwaum lik a convict, dowf and dour
As the runt o a riven aik
Whaur ghouls can sit or their hurdies ache.

The westlins sun, reid owre "The Gowf,"
Fluids the Links wi glaumerie,
I sit we ma bogles dour and dowf,
Idleness and Malancolie;
Lik a braw new penny Sol dwines doun
Fou like ma hert—but the saul toom.

We Shall Never Want

Och, we shall never want, witch, you and I,
The gowd that is hairt's richest tresorie—
Come aa the hazards that on Eros tend
We hae a gowden hoard put bye
   —A million in memorie.

Dailie, weeklie, we brenn aa the bonds
And princelie squander luve til the fowr airts
Yet dailie, weeklie, it itsel renews
For ase o spendthrift luve is Eros' gowd
   —Luve's queerest alchemie.

Tho we want muckle and want maistlie time
—In time we're trulie beggars o the bluid—
Yet aa o time is ours and will be aye.
For us the naitural laws suspend:
   —Is pairt o the tresorie.

Och, we shall never want, witch, you and I,
Tho we be gangrels born and broken men
Our private mint's in Aphrodite's kist
And sae our credit's bundless as the main
   —Sae rich, witch, are we.

The Grace of God and the Meth-Drinker

There ye gang, ye daft
And doitit dotterel, ye saft
Crazed outland skalrag saul
In your bits and ends o winnockie duds
Your fyled and fozie-fousome clouts
As fou's a fish, crackt and craftie-drunk
Wi bleerit reid-rimmed
Ee and slaveran crozie mou
Dwaiblan owre the causie like a ship
Storm-toss't i' the Bay of Biscay O
At-sea indeed and hauf-seas-owre
Up-til-the-thrapple's-pap
Or up-til-the-crosstrees-sunk—
    Wha kens? Wha racks?

Hidderie-hetterie stouteran in a dozie dwaum
O' ramsh reid-biddie—Christ!
  The stink
O' jake ahint him, a mephitic
Rouk o miserie, like some unco exotic
Perfume o the Orient no juist sae easilie tholit
By the bleak barbarians o the Wast
But subtil, acrid, jaggan the nebstrous
Wi'n owrehailan ugsome guff, maist delicat,
Like in scent til the streel o a randie gib. . . .
    O-hone-a-ree!

His toothless gums, his lips, bricht cramasie
A schere-bricht slash o bluid
A schene like the leaman gleid o rubies
Throu the gray-white stibble
O' his blank unrazit chafts, a hangman's
Heid, droolie wi gob, the bricht een
Sichtless, cannie, blythe, and slee—
             Unkennan.

Ay,
    Puir gangrel!
                There
—But for the undeemous glorie and grace
O' a mercifu omnipotent majestic God
Superne eterne and sceptred in the firmament
Whartil the praises o the leal rise
Like incense aye about Your throne,
Ayebydan, thochtless, and eternallie hauf-drunk
Wi nectar, Athole-brose, ambrosia—nae jake for You—
                                God, there!—
But for the 'bunesaid unsocht grace, unprayed for,
Undeserved—
        Gangs,
                Unregenerate,
                      Me.

To Li Po[1] in the Delectable Mountains of Tien-Mu[2] In Memoriam Robert Fergusson[3] in the Blythfu Fields Frae the Auk[4] in Auld Reekie

An ourie nicht was yesternicht,
Li Po, sir, in Auld Reekie here.
Dooms cauld it was,
Cauld as the Viking hell,
Boozan doun the Royal Mile
The hinder-end o Februar
Month o fevers
    (As, Sir Precentor,[5] ye'll mynd weill);
The drowie haar
Like icie mouswabs
Hung in the airn streets;
No monie folk abraid; and the lamps

Glauman out like loom-bund ships. . . .
At the Canongate fuit,
Lichtless and silent as a jail
The great Palace sleepit.
But in the bar
Outby across the road
By Mary's Bath-tub, aa
Was cantie, snog, and bricht,
A cheerie howff, and a crousie companie
O' philosophers and tinks—Aa
'Scholards an' gennemen, beGode!'

—A wee thing douncome i' the world maybe
But nane the waur o yon,
I'd hae ye ken.
A man's a man!
  And has, forbye,
  Belike as nocht,
  A near-in cousin
  In the ministrie
  Or medicine, teachin,
  Or the law—ay, *law*!
  —Jungle law, o course—
  Or maybe's a collegiate
  Professor (juist)
  In some ither deeper mysterie
  —As 'Real Auld Scotch'
  Or 'Cute wee hures',
  Petrol, fags, or nylons. . . .
    Etcetera. . . .
  Och, man, ye ken it aa!
Ay, a crousie companie, a cheerie howff
And the whiskie was liquid ingots,
Dauds o the purest gowd!
—Like Darnley's broider't wallicoat
There hingan on the waa.

*

Hamewith, up the brae, we sang
As we were student callants aince again.
The dour nicht was rent!
The cobbles, skinklan, rang
Wi our busteous bellochin!
Frae Abbeymount houlit the muezzin:
'*La' Allah illa Allah!*'
And his prophet Pate Mahoun
There wi us in the flesh
Ay, Auld Bairdie, in the midst.

Frae the dim Palace
Throu the mist
Juist ae wee yalla licht
Glink't like a lewd auld procuress.

Hola! Hola!
Up and bar the door,
Douce burgesses my dears!
There's reivers on the toun the-nicht!
Guaird weill your liquor
And your dochters pure
For the Terrible Turk is near
With Ivan Skavinski Skavour
And eke the Bulbul Ameer!
–Turn doun a cup for Saki, tae!
And for Li Po, the Auk, guid sir,
And the gowden Horde
O' Hippogriphs, Hughs, Seceders and Hectors,
Rab the Ranter and Rab Sir Precentor,
Clunie and the Hunter Bard
–Shennachies aa, aa shennachies, by Gar!
O mercifu Lord, hou lang, hou lang?
And a lean auld faggot Wullie Dunbar
Black as the Enemie his-sel
Hirplan alang wi girn and greit
And a tongue as rouch as the Tron Kirk Bell.

–Ay, we were a wirricow weirdlike thrang,
A touzie tregallion o tykes indeed.

In the Palace, doun ablow,
The ae lane yalla licht aye glents,
Glinkan like a coorse Madame–
And damn the delyte has she in-ben!

–Whiles, looman throu the wreithes,
Phantasmagorical,
The muckle dowp o Arthur's Seat
Hull-doun til the elements–
'Maist symbolical!'
Says Smairtie. '*Lyon-hurdies*, by the Rude!'
'The saul o Scotland sleepan sound!'
–Aiblins. Maybe. Ye could be richt;
I wadna ken, at that. . . .
But hae my douts.

The nicht was ourie richt eneuch;
But nocht we felt the drowie rouk
Bane-cauld, or the weet–or ocht
Ither, as I can mynd–
Hamewith mirrilie up the brae
Wi a hauf-mutchkin and hip-pint
And screwtap chasers clinkum-clankum
In tune wi our maist important bletherin,
Our maist significant piss-and-wind . . .
   –While the world in its daith-dance
   Skuddert and spun
   In the haar and wind o space and time . . .
   Wi nane to accolad the goddess-mune,
   Invisible, but her foredoomed elect:
The bards, the drouths, the daft, the luvers,
We!
–Ay, here was aa wir companie,
Tinks and philosophers,
True Servants o the Queen.

*

134

Ay, weill ye'll mynd, Sir Precentor, sir!
It was a guid nicht was yesternicht,
And a guid nicht, tae, in memorie
  (Tho deil the moral that I can see)
Li Po, man, by the Yalla River
Twal hunder year bygane and mair
'Wildeie drinkan alane by munelicht!'
—I salute ye, sir!
Wi Rab, mine auld familiar,
Born twa centures syne, this year,
—A thousand younger nor ye, auld makar . . .
Guidsakes, and I thocht, a moment, we three
Were on the bash thegither!
As weill micht be, I hope, here-efter.

—Guidnicht, then, for the nou,
    Li Po,
In the Blythefu Hills o Tien-Mu.

Hamewith

'En ma fin est mon commencement.'—Marie Stuart.

Man at the end
Til the womb wends,
Fisher to sea,
Hunter to hill,
Miner the pit seeks,
Sodjer the bield.

As bairn on breist
Seeks his first need
Makar his thocht prees,
Doer his deed,
Sanct his peace
And sinner remeid.

Man in dust is lain
And exile wins hame.

R. CROMBIE SAUNDERS

The Empty Glen

Time ticks away the centre of my pride
Emptying its glen of cattle, crops, and song,
Till its deserted headlands are alone
Familiar with the green uncaring tide.

What gave this land to gradual decay?
The rocky field where plovers make their nest
Now undisturbed had once the soil to raise
A happy people, but from day to day

The hamlets failed, the young men sought the towns,
Bewildered age looked from the cottage door
Upon the wreck of all they'd laboured for,
The rotting gate, the bracken on the downs;

And wondered if the future was so black
The children would have stayed but did not dare,
Who might, they hoped, be happy where they are.
And wondered, Are they ever coming back?

TOM SCOTT

Sea-Dirge

I found him drowned on the rock that night
And the wind high; moonlight it was
And the hungry sucking of the sea
At my feet, stretching away in front of me.
Never a lover was laid on the braes that night
Nor any living soul I'm thinking, unless they were mad
And drawn to the moon. I found him there
In the rocks that night and the wind was high;

Bare he was as the sea and the rock, on either side,
With a rag of silk in his hand
And sand in his nose; moonlight it was
And the sea before me: my hair dragged at my eyes.

I couldn't see, but a hand of ice was plunged
Deep in my womb, I found him lying
Drowned on the rock that night and
The wind was high; moonlight it was
And the sea sucked at my feet.
Then I heard from the cave behind
The skirl of the piper who died on rocks,
The wail of the pipes and then the cry of his soul.
I upped and screamed at the wind and the sea,
I stripped my forsaken breasts to the moon
And I kissed the frost of his mouth and the sand.
I found him drowned on the rock that night
And the wind high; moonlight it was
And the hungry sucking of the sea
At my feet and his clammy head in my breasts
That were bare as the rock and the sea and the sand.

Night Song

The moon is high and at the full
And under that hypnotic gaze
Held in magical control
The world is frozen motionless.
Every star is in its place.

From her principality
Venus swoops behind the line
Of the horizon, quietly
As the deeper night sets in;
And stepping with a wayward grace

From her cave among the stars
Night herself plucks off her dress,
Slips from each silken thing that mars
Her beauty and her loveliness,
To tremble in the winds that press

Coldly on her drowsy skin.
And bold with desire comes stealthy up
And creeps unbidden naked in
To my empty breast, as in a cup
A cool wine's rousing kiss.

On my ribs her head's impressed.
Voluptuously her cold loins
Belly and her laden breast
Lie against my restless limbs
Drawing up a sea's distress

In one spear of desire; I am held
Thus, polarised, compressed,
But from that hymened echo exiled
Forever; held; the cold mist
Of the halfling world upon my face.

But held so delicately love
That if you come not presently
To prove this night, I fear the glove
Of mind will fall entirely from me
To rot among the silent grass.

Auld Sanct-Aundrians — Brand the Builder

On winter days, about the gloamin hour,
Whan the knock on the college touer
Is chappan lowsin-time,
And ilka mason packs his mell and tools awa

Ablow his banker, and bien forenenst the waa
The labourer haps the lave o the lime
Wi soppan secks, to keep it frae a frost, or faa
O suddent snaw
Duran the nicht,
And scrawnie craws flap in the shell-green licht
Towards yon bane-bare rickle o trees
That heeze
Up on the knowe abuin the toun,
And the red goun
Is happan mony a student frae the snell nor-easter,
Malcolm Brand, the maister,
Seean the last hand thru the yett
Afore he bars and padlocks it,
Taks ae look round his stourie yaird
Whaur chunks o stane are liggan
Like the ruins o some auld-farrant biggin:
Picks a skelf out o his beard,
Scliffs his tackety buits and syne
Clunters hamelins doun the wyn'.

Alang the shore,
The greinan white sea-owsen ramp and roar.

The main street echoes back his clinkan fuit-faas
Frae its waas,
Whaur owre the kerb and causeys yellow licht
Presses back the mirk nicht
As shop fronts flüde the pavin-stanes in places,
Like the peintit faces
Whures pit on, or actresses,—ay, or meenisters—
To please their several customers.
But aye the nordren nicht, cauld as rumour,
Taks command,
Chills the toun wi his militarie humour,
And plots his map o starns wi deadly hand.

Doun by the sea,
Murns the white swaw owre the wrack ayebydanlie.

Stoupan throu the anvil pend
Gaes Brand,
And owre the coort wi the twa-three partan creels,
The birss air fu
o the smell o the sea, and fish, and meltit glue,
Draws up at his door, and syne,
Hawkan his craig afore he gangs in ben,
Gies a bit scrape at the grater wi his heels.

The kail-pat on the hob is hotteran fu
O the usual hash o Irish stew,
And by the grate, a red-haired bewtie frettit thin,
His wife is kaain a spurtle round.
He swaps his buits for his baffies but a sound.
The twa-three bairnies ken to mak nae din
Whan faither's in,
And sit on creepies round about.
Brand gies a muckle yawn, and howks his paper out.

Tither side the fire,
The kettle sings like a telephone wire.

'Lord, for what we are about to receive
Help us to be tryly thankful—Aimen—
Wumman, ye've pit ingans in't again.'

'Gae wa ye coorse auld hypocrite!
Thank the Lord for your maet, syne grue at it!'

Wi chowks drawn ticht in a speakless sconner
He glowers on her:
Syne on the quate and straucht-faced bairns:
Faulds his paper doun by his eatin-airns,
And, til the loud tick-tockan o the knock,
Sups, and reads, wi nae ither word nor look.

The warld outside
Like a lug-held sea-shell, roars wi the rinnan tide.

The supper owre, Brand redds up for the nicht.
Aiblins there's a schedule for to price,
Or somethin nice
On at the picters—sacont hoose—
Or some poleetical meetin wants his licht,
Or aiblins, wi him t-total aa his life,
No able to seek the pub to flee the wife,
Daunders out the West Sands 'on the loose'.
Whatever tis,
The waater slorps frae his elbucks as he synds his phiz.

And this is aa the life he kens there is.

MAURICE LINDSAY

On Seeing a Picture o Johann Christian Fischer in The National Gallery, Edinburgh

Johann Christian Fischer? Mm—the face is kindly,
the wig weil-snod, the features firmly set,
as leanan on a harpsichord by Albrecht,
wi quill in haun you scrieve a menuet.

The feet sae carefully crossed tae shaw the buckl't shuinn,
gimp hose and curly cravat o white lace,
the fiddle on the chair, the music heaped—
the hail, a glisk of Eighteenth Century grace!

Gin ony o your stately airs and tunefu dances
that kittl't pouther't duchesses lang syne,
culd tinkle oot o Albrecht's yalla keyboard,
maist folk 'ud luik at you a second time.

But aa is dusty silence, like the derk ahint you,
and e'en your notes are naething but a blur;
the background, fu o shaddaws, seems tae draw you
tae hap you in its aa-embracan slur.

Yet there you staun oot still, by Gainsborough made immortal,
as gin sic fame was shairly jist your due—
a perfect shell upon the shore left strandit,
a piece for antiquarians tae view.

Farm Widow

She moved among the sour smell of her hens' droppings,
her cheeks rubbed to a polish, her skirts bustled
with decent pride; alone since the day the tractor
hauled itself up the field on the hill and toppled

her man away from her. Around her feet
her daughter played, the face of innocence puckered
with the solemn self-importance of being alone
in a grown-up world; her friends, the hens that speckled

her mother's allotment. Some of the weekly folk
who came to buy their eggs, had watched her counting
their change from the money smooth in her purse, and given her
silent pity, then sensed that she wasn't wanting

in anything they could offer; that she seemed
like one whom life had used too soon for writing
some sort of purpose with, her gestures economies
spelling completeness; gone beyond our waiting

for times and places to happen, beyond the will,
to where time and place lie colourless and still.

At the Mouth of the Ardyne

The water rubs against itself,
glancing many faces at me.
One winces as the dropped fly
tears its tension. Then it heals.

Being torn doesn't matter.
The water just goes on saying
all that water has to say,
what the dead come back to.

Then a scar opens.
Something of water is ripped out,
a struggle with swung air.
I batter it on a loaf of stone.

The water turns passing faces,
innumerable pieces of silver.
I wash my hands, pack up, and
go home wishing I hadn't come.

Later, I eat my guilt.

A Picture of the Caledonian Hunt

Over their fences with superb aplomb
these claret-blooded hunting gentry soar,
their leathering women, mistresshood confirmed
by hourglass stays, and half their years to pour

unquestioned dominance down, curbed in and held
above the silence of their last *halloo*,
kept from oblivion by the picture's edge
that scuffed their breathless quarry out of view.

Why did they ride to hounds? Some need to assert
the blood's uncertainty, their rulership
of field and ditch? Or, like the pounded fox,
hopeful they'd give their warmest fears the slip?

Or did they straddle stallions to exult
and stretch those instincts men and horses share,
the satisfaction straining thews and sinews
relax into the sense of use and wear?

Did movement threaten from behind scrubbed hedges,
the spring of winter coiled in frosted mould
mock at their privilege, or seem to trap them
nearer the thicket of their growing old?

They exist for ever; lonely, frozen gestures,
the life they leaped at and were ground to, thawed
beneath them; gone with all they thought they stood for.
Yet were they further from whatever flowed

as clarity around their consciousness,
wearing away what living seemed to mean,
but somehow never did, than we are who
catch half-familiar glimpses of it, seen

as landscape poured out by a 'plane is; clean
in its detachment, of itself complete?
What we are left with here are the blanched stains
imprinting lineaments of a defeat

not different from ours, but doubly separated:
by the unexplorable gography
of time, each of us on our island of it
misted about in our own difficulty.

Picking Apples

Apple time, and the trees brittle with fruit.
My children climb the bent, half-sapping branches
to where the apples, cheeked with the hectic flush
of Autumn, hang. The children bark their haunches

and lean on the edge of their balance. The apples are out
of reach; so they shake the tree. Through a tussle of leaves and
   laughter
the apples thud down; thud on the orchard grasses
in rounded, grave finality, each one after

the other dropping; the muffled sound of them dropping
like suddenly hearing the beats of one's own heart
falling away, as if shaken by some storm
as localised as this. Loading them into the cart,

the sweet smell of their bruises moist in the sun,
their skins' bloom tacky against the touch,
I experience fulfilment, suddenly aware
of some ripe, wordless answer, knowing no such

answers exist; only questions, questions, the beating years,
the dropped apples . . . the kind of touch and go
that poetry makes satisfactions of;
reality, with nothing more to show

than a brush of branches, time and the apples falling,
and shrill among the leaves, children impatiently calling.

Seagulls

Throats of cloud hoarse with spume,
flexing a wings'-breadth of unease,
or, scanning nearer, shrugs of shoulder
in imitation of the sea's.

Seagulls . . . seamaws . . . bellies of ocean . . .
Fishermen wear them round the stoop
of backs bent to the nets. Flicking
eyes that hook and reel-in their swoop

to rip the living water's guts,
clip bread from hands, or seize scraps
of fading entrails limp in the smell
of their own decay. White paps

puffed on bollards against the wind's
huffing, or hunched like age on rocks,
or tossed in sudden unfurled panic,
the singleness of their cry mocks

the syllables we shape as words.
For we can't make sounds that say
nothing of love or hate; only
uncalculating necessity.

Love's Anniversaries

It was the generosity of delight
that first we learned in a sparsely-furnished flat
clothed in our lovers' nakedness. By night
we timidly entered what we marvelled at,

ranging the flesh's compass. But by day
we fell together, fierce with awkwardness
that window-light and scattered clothing lay
impassive round such urgent happiness.

Now, children, years and many rooms away,
and tired with experience, we climb the stairs
to our well-furnished room; undress, and say
familiar words for love; and from the cares

that back us, turn together and once more seek
the warmth of wonder each to the other meant
so strong ago, and with known bodies speak
the unutterable language of content.

DONALD MACRAE

The Pterodactyl and Powhatan's Daughter

American poets have seen their country
as a brown girl lying serene in the sun,
as Powhatan's daughter with open thighs,
her belly a golden plain of wheat,
her breasts the firm and fecund hills,
each sinuous vein a river, and in each wrist
    the pulse of cataracts.

She has rejected no lover, not the
fanatic English nor the hungry Scot,
the trading Dutchman nor the industrious
continental peasant, used to oppression,
the patent stolen negro nor the
laborious Asiatic, schooled to diligent,
    ingenious labour.

By all her lovers she has been fruitful,
has multiplied all numbers, lying
indolent, calm and almost asleep,
only her lake-eyes watchful, expectant
of new wanderers from further shores
seeking her young immortal body,
    waiting unsated.

She is patient this girl with her black hair tumbled,
with her earth-bedded, receptive body stretched,
relaxed and leisured, at ease in the sun.

In her veins the sun-warm blood is coursing,
swift running through the golden body,
obedient to the steadfast heart's command.
    the unending beat.

Not such is our land. It is a skeleton
crushed by the long weight of years, the bone
hard stone, the skin tight on the sinew,
the flesh wasted by long years of hunger.
It is a stone land, a hard land of bone,
of lean muscle and atrophied membrane
    ridged over ribs.

This is a pterodactyl land,
lean survivor of ice and the frost,
sea and the parching sun, which,
the last of its kind, is now dying
by inches, blinking and bleeding through the
death shroud of mist, the dissolving film
    of steady rain.

We dwell on the stiffening corpse of Scotland,
starved lice on a pauper's body
chill on a marble slabl Should we leave?
Should we follow our father's pattern,
make love to Powhatan's daughter,
westward refurrow the weary sea?
    We had better not.

She too is a myth: we'd be wise to forget
our symbols, turn from the romantic vision,
the loose-thought personified images of countries,
to study and learn to read, painfully,
the facts of these matters aright, then nourish—
if we have heart—some slight sober hope
    of tomorrow.

SYDNEY TREMAYNE

The Falls of Falloch

This white explosion of water plunges down
With the deep-voiced rush of sound that shakes a city.
A fine cold smoke drifts across dripping stone
And wet black walls of rock shut in the scene.

Now thought hangs sheer on a precipice of beauty
Lifting with leaping water out from the rock.
A gasp of time, flung clear in a weight of falling,
Bursts like a bud above the deep pool's black
Parted and curled back under by the shock
Where light's bright spark dives to the dark's controlling.

But the brilliance is not extinguished. The heart leaps up,
The heart of the fall leaps up, an eternal explosion,
Force without spending, form without fetter of shape.
And at the pool's edge wavelets scarcely lap
Where drifted spume clings with a soft adhesion.

Remote Country

The way goes snaking upward through the heat.
Out of the carving river's narrow space
Shaken with noise of water, black and white,
You climb at last into a scooped out place
Where nothing moves but wind treading grass.

All cover's past. Below, the waterfalls
Dig out of sight, like memory. You stare up,
Strange in this trap ringed all about by hills,
To find the one way out, confined and steep,
Watched by whatever eyes look from the top.

When you have crossed the open, reached the height,
It is a brown plateau, cratered and bare,
Low, lumpy hills and black, eroded peat
Stretching as far as light can throw its glare,
No living thing in sight in sky or moor.

Mind finds its way to meet with solitude.
Bear this in mind: the image will not age
Of desert, light and always moving cloud.
It is a vision to exhaust all rage
Calculate nothing. Leave an empty page.

North of Berwick

Slowly the sea is parted from the sky:
The light surprises, crinkling on the water.
The white sun hardens; cliffs solidify.
A long coast of red rock where three swans fly
Engraves itself in calm, deceptive weather.

Three swans fly north, a diesel thumping south
Draws out of sight along the rusting railway,
All windows clouded with a communal breath.
Fields flash in the sunlight, far beneath
The sea turns in its scales, well in a seal's way.

No boat invades that shining emptiness.
Because the waves are distant, the sky windless,
That pale line round the shore looks motionless.
Hearing such border warfare lost in space
You say the breathing of the sea is endless.

What is the one thing constant? Can you say?
The loneliness that we are born to merges
Perhaps with such a place on such a day.
No stones cry out because we cannot stay.
Through all our absences the long tide surges.

ALEXANDER SCOTT

Recipe: To Mak a Ballant

To mak a ballant:
tak onie image sclents frae the dark o your mind,
sieve it through twal years' skill
i the fewest words can haud it
(meantime steeran in your hert's bluid),
spice wi wit, saut wi passion,
bile i the hettest fire your love can kindle,
and serve at the scaud in your strangmaist stanza
(the haill process aa to be dune at aince)

Syne rin like hell afore the result explodes!

Scrievin

I walkit air, I walkit late
By craigs o gloamin-coloured stane,
I heard the sea-maws skirl and keen
Like sclate-pens scraichan ower a sclate.

I walkit late, I walkit air
By parks that winter smairged wi snaw,
I saw the spoor o pad and claw
Like ink on paper prentit there.

I lippened syne, I lookit syne,
But cudna comprehend ava
A word o what I heard or saw
Scrievit by hands sae unlike mine.

Haar in Princes Street

The heicht o the biggins is happit in rauchens o haar,
   The statues alane
  Stand clearly, heid til fit in stane,
And lour frae *then* and *thonder* at *hencefurth* and *here.*

The past on pedestals, girnan frae ilka feature,
   Wi granite frouns
  They glower at the present's feckless loons,
Its gangrels tint i the haar that fankles the future.

The fowk o flesh, stravaigan wha kens whither,
   And come frae whar,
  Hudder like ghaists i the gastrous haar,
Forfochten and wae i the smochteran smore o the weather.

They swaiver and flirn i the freeth like straes i the sea,
   An airtless swither,
  Steeran awa the t'ane frae t'ither,
Alane, and lawlie aye tae be lanesome sae.

But heich i the lift (whar the haar is skailan fairlie
   In blufferts o wind)
  And blacker nor nicht whan starns are blind,
The Castle looms, a fell, a fabulous ferlie.

Dragonish, darksome, dourlie grapplan the Rock
   Wi claws o stane
  That scart our historie bare til the bane,
It braks like Fate throu Time's wanchancy reek.

Continent o Venus

She lies ablow my body's lust and love,
A country dearly-kent, and yet sae fremd
That she's at aince thon Tir-nan-Og I've dreamed,
The airt I've lived in, whar I mean tae live,

And mair, much mair, a mixter-maxter warld
Whar fact and dream are taigled up and snorled.

I ken ilk bay o aa her body's strand,
Yet ken them new ilk time I come to shore,
For she's the uncharted sea whar I maun fare
To find anither undiscovered land,
To find it fremd, and yet to find it dear,
To seek for't aye, and aye be bydan there.

Evensong

I

As I bent to the typewriter, clattering clattering keys,
The window was open before me and dusk was falling
Across the meadows and glooming the green of trees
While over the twilight early owls were calling.
Or so they told me—I neither saw nor heard,
Intent on letters, until the work was ended,
When, as I lifted my head and relaxed, a bird
In song outside made evening suddenly splendid.

II

Such moments once, a dazzle of revelation,
Would dagger the heart defenceless. Now I listened
Without a wound, accepting the song I was given,
Content to accept it as song, the years gone over
When sight of a seagull's swoop upon grey water
Or petals fluttering butterfly-bright from flowers
Could solve at a stroke the puzzle of all existence.
I heard the song and was glad. And it proved nothing.

Cat and King

A cat may look at a king–
Oh, fairly that!
But a king can swack the heid
Frae onie cat.

The heid may look at a king
Wi gloweran een–
But little's the guid o thon
Whan naething's seen!

DERICK THOMSON

Clann-Nighean An Sgadain

An gàire mar chraiteachan salainn
ga fhroiseadh bho 'm bial,
an sàl 's am picil air an teanga,
's na miaran cruinne, goirid a dheanadh giullachd,
no a thogadh leanabh gu socair, cuimir,
seasgair, fallain,
gun mhearachd,
's na sùilean cho domhainn ri fèath.

B'e bun-os-cionn na h-eachdraidh a dh' fhàg iad
'nan tràillean aig ciùrairean cutach,
thall 's a-bhos air Galldachd 's an Sasuinn.
Bu shaillte an duais a thàrr iad
ás na mìltean bharaillean ud,
gaoth na mara geur air an craiceann,
is eallach a' bhochdainn 'nan ciste,
is mara b'e an gàire
shaoileadh tu gu robh an teud briste.

Ach bha craiteachan uaille air an cridhe,
ga chumail fallain,
is bheireadh cutag an teanga
slisinn á fanaid nan Gall–
agus bha obair rompa fhathast
nuair gheibheadh iad dhachaidh,
ged nach biodh maoin ac':
air oidhche robach gheamhraidh,
ma bha sud an dàn dhaibh,
dheanadh iad daoine.

The Herring Girls

From the Gaelic of Derick Thomson
(*English version by Derick Thomson*)

Their laughter like a sprinkling of salt
showered from their lips,
brine and pickle on their tongues,
and the stubby short fingers that could handle fish,
or lift a child gently, neatly, safely, wholesomely,
unerringly,
and the eyes that were as deep as a calm.

The topsy-turvy of history had made them
slaves to short-arsed curers,
here and there in the Lowlands, in England.
Salt the reward they won
from those thousands of barrels,
the sea-wind sharp on their skins,
and the burden of poverty in their kists,
and were it not for their laughter
you might think the harp-string was broken.

But there was a sprinkling of pride in their hearts,
keeping them sound,
and their tongues' gutting-knife

155

would tear a strip from the Lowlanders' mockery —
and there was work awaiting them
when they got home,
though they had no wealth:
on a wild winter's night,
if that were their lot,
they would make men.

Cruaidh?

Cuil-lodair, is Briseadh na h-Eaglaise,
is briseadh nan tacannan—
lamhachas-làidir dà thrian de ar comas;
'se seòltachd tha dhìth oirnn.
Nuair a theirgeas a' chruaidh air faobhar na speala
caith bhuat a' chlach-lìomhaidh;
chan eil agad ach iarunn bog
mur eil de chruas 'nad innleachd na ni sgathadh.

Is caith bhuat briathran mìne
oir chan fhada bhios briathran agad;
tha Tuatha Dé Danann fo'n talamh,
tha Tìr nan Og anns an Fhraing,
's nuair a ruigeas tu Tìr a' Gheallaidh,
mura bi thu air t' aire,
coinnichidh Sasunnach riut is plìon air,
a dh' innse dhut gun tug Dia, bràthair athar, còir dha ás an fhearann.

Steel?

From the Gaelic of Derick Thomson
(*English version by Derick Thomson*)

Culloden, the Disruption,
and the breaking up of the tack-farms —
two thirds of our power is violence;
it is cunning we need.
When the tempered steel near the edge of the scythe-blade is worn,
throw away the whetstone;
you have nothing left but soft iron
unless your intellect has a steel edge that will cut clean.

And throw away soft words,
for soon you will have no words left;
the Tuatha De Danann[1] are underground,
the Land of the Ever-Young is in France,
and when you reach the Promised Land,
unless you are on your toes,
a bland Englishman will meet you,
and say to you that God, his uncle, has given him a title to the land.

EDWIN MORGAN

To Joan Eardley

Pale yellow letters
humbly straggling across
the once brilliant red
of a broken shop-face
CONFECTIO
and a blur of children
at their games, passing,

---

[1] *Tuatha De Danann* a supernatural race in Ireland, sometimes said to be the progenitors of the fairies.

gazing as they pass
at the blur of sweets
in the dingy, cosy
Rottenrow window—
an Eardley on my wall.
Such rags and streaks
that master us!—
that fix what the pick
and bulldozer have crumbled
to a dingier dust,
the living blur
fiercely guarding
energy that has vanished,
cries filling still
the unechoing close!
I wandered by the rubble
and the houses left standing
kept a chill, dying life
in their islands of stone.
No window opened
as the coal cart rolled
and the coalman's call
fell coldly to the ground.
But the shrill children
jump on my wall.

King Billy

Grey over Riddrie the clouds piled up,
dragged their rain through the cemetery trees.
The gates shone cold. Wind rose
flaring the hissing leaves, the branches
swung, heavy, across the lamps.
Gravestones huddled in drizzling shadow,
flickering streetlight scanned the requiescats,
a name and an urn, a date, a dove

picked out, lost, half regained.
What is this dripping wreath, blown from its grave
red, white, blue, and gold
'To Our Leader of Thirty Years Ago' –

Bareheaded, in dark suits, with flutes
and drums, they brought him here, in procession
seriously, King Billy of Brigton, dead,
from Bridgeton Cross: a memory of violence,
brooding days of empty bellies,
billiard smoke and a sour pint,
boots or fists, famous sherrickings,
the word, the scuffle, the flash, the shout,
bloody crumpling in the close,
bricks for papish windows, get
the Conks next time, the Conks ambush
the Billy Boys, the Billy Boys the Conks till
Sillitoe scuffs the razors down the stank –
No, but it isn't the violence they remember
but the legend of a violent man
born poor, gang-leader in the bad times
of idleness and boredom, lost in better days,
a bouncer in a betting club,
a quiet man at last, dying
alone in Bridgeton in a box bed.
So a thousand people stopped the traffic
for the hearse of a folk hero and the flutes
threw 'Onward Christian Soldiers' to the winds
from unironic lips, the mourners kept
in step, and there were some who wept.

Go from the grave. The shrill flutes
are silent, the march dispersed.
Deplore what is to be deplored,
and then find out the rest.

Aberdeen Train

Rubbing a glistening circle
on the steamed-up window I framed
a pheasant in a field of mist.
The sun was a great red thing somewhere low,
struggling with the milky scene. In the furrows
a piece of glass winked into life,
hypnotized the silly dandy; we
hooted past him with his head cocked,
contemplating a bottle-end.
And this was the last of October,
a Chinese moment in the Mearns.

Good Friday

Three o'clock. The bus lurches
round into the sun. 'D's this go–'
he flops beside me–'right along Bath Street?
–Oh tha's, tha's all right, see I've
got to get some Easter eggs for the kiddies.
I've had a wee drink, ye understand–
ye'll maybe think it's a–funny day
to be celebratin–well, no but ye see
I wasny workin–I don't say it's right
I'm no sayin it's right, ye understand–ye understand?
But anyway tha's the way I look at it–
I'm no borin you, eh?–ye see today,
take today, I don't know what today's in aid of,
whether Christ was–crucified or was he–
rose fae the dead like, see what I mean?
You're an educatit man, you can tell me–
–Aye, well. There ye are. It's been seen
time and again, the workin man
has nae education, he jist canny–jist
hasny got it, know what I mean,

he's jist bliddy ignorant—Christ aye,
bliddy ignorant. Well—' The bus brakes violently,
he lunges for the stair, swings down—off,
into the sun for his Easter eggs,
on very
       nearly
          steady
            legs.

GEORGE MACKAY BROWN

The Old Women

Go sad or sweet or riotous with beer
Past the old women gossiping by the hour,
They'll fix on you from every close and pier
An acid look to make your veins run sour.

'No help,' they say, 'his grandfather that's dead
Was troubled with the same dry-throated curse,
And many a night he made the ditch his bed.
This blood comes welling from the same cracked source.'

On every kind of merriment they frown.
But I have known a gray-eyed sober boy
Sail to the lobsters in a storm, and drown.
Over his body dripping on the stones
Those same old hags would weave into their moans
An undersong of terrible holy joy.

The Lodging

The stones of the desert town
Flush; and, a star-filled wave,
Night steeples down.

From a pub door here and there
A random ribald song
Leaks on the air.

The Roman in a strange land
Broods, wearily leaning
His lance in the sand.

The innkeeper over the fire
Counting his haul, hears not
The cry from the byre;

But rummaging in the till
Grumbles at the drunken shepherds
Dancing on the hill;

And wonders, pale and grudging,
If the queer pair below
Will pay their lodging.

Trout Fisher

Semphill, his hat stuck full of hooks
   Sits drinking ale
      Among the English fishing visitors,
    Probes in detail
        Their faults in casting, reeling, selection of flies.
'Never,' he urges, 'do what it says in the books.'
     Then they, obscurely wise,

Abandon by the loch their dripping oars
And hang their throttled tarnish on the scale.

'Forgive me, every speckled trout,'
    Says Semphill then,
        'And every swan and eider on these waters.
    Certain strange men,
        Taking advantage of my poverty
Have wheedled all my subtle loch-craft out
        So that their butchery
        Seem find technique in the ear of wives and daughters;
And I betray the loch for a white coin.'

Wedding

With a great working of elbows
The fiddlers ranted
            —Joy to Ingrid and Magnus!

With much boasting and burning
The whisky circled
            —Wealth to Ingrid and Magnus!

With deep clearings of the throat
The minister intoned
            —Thirdly, Ingrid and Magnus. . . .

Ingrid and Magnus stared together
When midnight struck
At a white unbroken bed.

Stromness Market

They drove to the Market with ringing pockets.
   Folster found a girl
Who put wounds on his face and throat,
Small diagonal wounds like red doves.
   Johnstone stood beside the barrel.
All day he stood there.
He woke in a ditch, his mouth full of ashes.
   Grieve bought a balloon and a goldfish.
He swung through the air.
He fired shotguns, rolled pennies, ate sweet fog from a stick.
   Heddle was at the Market also.
I know nothing of his activities.
He is and always was a quiet man.
   Garson fought three rounds with a negro boxer
And received thirty shillings,
Much applause, and an eye loaded with thunder.
   Where did they find Flett?
They found him in a brazen ring
Of blood and fire, a new Salvationist.
   A gipsy saw in the hand of Halcro
Great strolling herds, harvests, a proud woman.
He wintered in the poorhouse.

They drove home from the Market, under the stars,
Except for Johnstone
Who lay in a ditch, his mouth full of dying fires.

Old Fisherman with Guitar

A formal exercise for withered fingers.
   The head is bent,
     The eyes half closed, the tune
Lingers

And beats, a gentle wing the west had thrown
Against his breakwater wall with salt
                                    savage lament.

So fierce and sweet the song on the plucked string,
    Know now for truth
        These hands have cut from the net
The strong
        Crab-eaten corpse of Jock washed from a boat
One old winter, and gathered the mouth of Thora
                                    to his mouth.

The Poet

Therefore he no more troubled the pool of silence
But put on mask and cloak,
Strung a guitar
And moved among the folk.
Dancing they cried,
'Ah, how our sober islands
Are gay again, since this blind lyrical tramp
Invaded the Fair!'

Under the last dead lamp
When all the dancers and masks had gone inside
His cold stare
Returned to its true task, interrogation of silence.

BURNS SINGER

A Letter

Tonight I'll meet you: yes, tonight. I know
There are, perhaps, a thousand miles–but not
Tonight. Tonight I go inside. I take
All the walls down, the bric-a-brac, the trash,
The tawdry pungent dust these months have gathered
Into a heap about me. I must prepare
And somehow move away from the slow world,
The circling menace with its throat and teeth
Attempting definition; and brush off
Those thoughts that, clinging like thin fallen hairs,
Make me unclean; for I must go tonight
And, secret from my shadow, go alone
Back to the hour when you yourself became
So much my own that even my own eyes
Seemed strange compared to you who were a new
Complete pervasive organ of all sense
Through which I saw and heard and more than touched
The very dignity of experience.

Tree

Tree. Tree. Do you want to become a man?
A woman then? A wren in your branches?
You, tree, who stand stiller than I can,
   Do you want to move?
To flicker away from me, safely and swiftly away,
   Then slacken up to say:–
You are mine; I am yours? O tree, do you want to love?

You stand, tree, in the thick grass,
Upright, unquenchably still. A man passes.
But you, tree, stand still, and still as stained glass
   Gather the light

In a green bouquet, gather it up and spill
    Shadows about you until
With a dark splash like a beacon I wade in your night.

    Then I look up, tree, from at your feet:
    Sunlight splits into a shrapnel pattern;
    Leaves become black and the black leaves meet
        In layers on air.
Tenderly frisking, yet stubborn under the wind,
    And stubbornly in my mind
Remaining delicate though your black boughs glare.

    I think, thus looking, that perhaps some gnomes
    In buried places where they are homely
    Must busily, when the sky becomes
        Top-heavy with light,
Lift you up chirruping to its zenith and
    Brush the whole sky with green land
Till it looks like earth, earth photographed in flight.

    Or that the clouds, which frolic and glare,
    And sly as a weasel, furry, unfearing,
    Have let you down from their pleasant nowhere
        And bundled you high.
Tree. Tree. Symmetrical bonfire, igneous green,
    What did earth's heavens mean
When they let you fall then filled you with the sky?

    You do not care. You'll not be caring
    Whether or no it means that the queer
    Energy through you is disappearing
        With nothing more given,
That empty gravities from an empty earth
    Are throwing themselves through your girth
Until they can connect with empty heaven.

    Or, if you do, how can I tell,
    From the greedy cell where I guard myself

And count the worlds of me that kill
　　Neighbours with nearness,
How can I hope to understand you, tree,
　　You, the arch-stranger to me
Who cannot reach my own articulate clearness?

　　I stand beneath you and you build halls
　　Like filigreed cobwebs out of valleys
　　Or over my head where the slant light falls
　　　　You spill your sheaves
Of garnered shade about me, changing its
　　Brilliance to brilliance that splits
Leathery, lush, an involved aether of leaves.

　　I, the supreme animal, I man,
　　Dream up shapelier than the land
　　That nourishes you, or the sun can.
　　　　I who create
A mythology out of your driest twig, who can make
　　Your thickest timbers break,
I ask you to enter into my own estate.

　　Crouch your great body into this
　　Sweating sensitive skin, and listen:
　　These eyes watch, these lips kiss,
　　　　This heart breaks:
But you, for all your gusty lunges, can't
　　Even begin to want
The love that feeds you or the truth that takes.

　　You could have motion to teach you how
　　Nothing ever departs slowly:
　　You could have language itself to show
　　　　Why hope must fail:
And finally, climactic in your mind,
　　You'd know that you were blind
And other knowledge is impossible.

For I, as I stand sweetly here,
Look up at you and see you clearly
As one more thing I can't come near
     From above or below,
Discover you will never want to be
     Anything other than tree
And understand the thing I do not know.

     Yes. I am man. I cannot wish
Anything other than my own foolish
Need to change shape and so to brush
     The air like you
And shoot long roots beneath me into earth.
     I deny myself rebirth
By wishing to be born again anew.

     This play between us, you and me,
Proceeds by laws that bind us freely,
Me into man, you into tree,
     Together today.
There is a sufficient mystery here with you.
     Draw apart. We are two.
All this, all is sufficient. I go on my way.

     I move away downhill over lawns
Where the evening buttercup looks like dawning
Into a warm reply to the songs
     I suffer by.
You shake your birds' nests in the twilit wind.
     You do not follow my kind.
You stand, arms open to receive the sky.

ALASTAIR REID

Ghosts' Stories

That bull-necked blotch-faced farmer from Drumlore
would never dream (or so we heard him boast
to neighbours at the lamb sales in Kirkcudbright)
of paying the least attention to a ghost.

Were we to blame for teaching him a lesson?
We whored his daughter, spaded all his ewes,
brought a blight on his barley, drew the sea
rampaging over his sod . . .

If we had any doubt that deserved it,
that went when we heard him stamp his ruined acres
and blame it all on God.

When we went on and frightened Miss McQueen
for keeping children in on Halloween,
and wailed all night in the schoolhouse, she, poor woman,
sent for the Fire Brigade.
And so we made
fire lick from her hair, till they put her out.

The children knew what it was all about.

The Figures on the Frieze

Darkness wears off, and, dawning into light,
they find themselves unmagically together.
He sees the stains of morning in her face.
She shivers, distant in his bitter weather.

Diminishing of legend sets him brooding.
Great goddess-figures conjured from his book

170

blur what he sees with bafflement of wishing.
Sulky, she feels his fierce, accusing look.

Familiar as her own, his body's landscape
seems harsh and dull to her habitual eyes.
Mystery leaves, and, mercilessly flying,
the blind fiends come, emboldened by her cries.

Avoiding simple reach of hand for hand
(which would surrender pride) by noon they stand
withdrawn from touch, reproachfully alone,
small in each other's eyes, tall in their own.

Wild with their misery, they entangle now
in baffling agonies of why and how.
Afternoon glimmers, and they wound anew,
flesh, nerve, bone, gristle in each other's view.

'What have you done to me?' From each proud heart,
new phantoms walk in the deceiving air.
As the light fails, each is consumed apart,
he by his ogre vision, she by her fire.

When night falls, out of a despair of daylight,
they strike the lying attitudes of love,
and through the perturbation of their bodies,
each feels the amazing, murderous legends move.

Propinquity

is the province of cats. Living by accident,
lapping the food at hand, or sleeking down
in an adjacent lap when sleep occurs to them,
never aspiring to consistency
in homes or partners, unaware of property,
cats take their chances, love by need and nearness

as long as the need lasts, as long as the nearness
is near enough. The code of cats is simply
to take what comes. And those poor souls who claim
to own a cat, who long to recognize
in bland and narrowing eyes a look like love,
are bound to suffer should they expect
cats to come purring punctually home.
Home is only where the food and the fire are,
but might be anywhere. Cats fall on their feet,
nurse their own wounds, attend to their own laundry,
and purr at appropriate times. O folly, folly
to love a cat, and yet
we dress with love the distance that they keep,
the hair-raising way they have, and easily blame
all the abandoned litters and torn ears
on some marauding tiger. Well, no matter;
cats do not care.
    Yet part of us is cat. Confess—
love turns on accident, and needs
nearness; and the various selves we have
all come from our cat-wanderings, our chance
crossings. Imagination prowls at night,
cat-like among odd possibilities.
Only our dog-sense brings us faithfully homeward,
makes meaning out of accident, keeps faith,
and, cat-and-dog, the arguments go at it.
But every night, outside, cat-voices call
us out to take a chance, to leave
the safety of our baskets, and to let
what happens, happen. 'Live, live!' they catcall.
'Each moment is your next! Propinquity,
propinquity is all!'

To a Child at the Piano

Play the tune again; but this time
with more regard for the movement at the source of it,
and less attention to time. Time falls
curiously in the course of it.

Play the tune again; not watching
your fingering, but forgetting, letting flow
the sound till it surrounds you. Do not count
or even think. Let go.

Play the tune again; but try to be
nobody, nothing, as though the pace
of the sound were your heart beating, as though
the music were your face.

Play the tune again. It should be easier
to think less every time of the notes, of the measure.
It is all an arrangement of silence. Be silent, and then
play it for your pleasure.

Play the tune again; and this time, when it ends,
do not ask me what I think. Feel what is happening
strangely in the room as the sound glooms over
you, me, everything.

Now,
play the tune again.

W. PRICE TURNER

Homely Accommodation, Suit Gent

In that repository of auction pots and post-Ark
furniture, stepping over the creaking board
you always sprang another, setting Mrs Hagglebroth
ready to intercept you with her pleated smile
and plucked eyebrows up, while conducting her
wallpaper centenary festival with a stick of feathers.

In that saddlesoap atmosphere, there was no music
after Mozart, and no smoking in the dining-room.
Sunlight was discouraged: it fades the draperies.
Sunday papers she detested, like all dirt. Even
the bought earth was sterilised before the bulbs,
one to a pot, were planted; God rest their souls.

But the remarkable strain of slaughterhouse fly
that bloated its dipstick in her best insecticide
always escaped her notice, though she stiffened
at irregular movements of bedsprings, and blushed
when the cistern gargled openly. Somehow her gentlemen
kept moving on, though she prayed for them all.

It was as if, when the seed stirred in them, they
thought of her with rubber gloves on, oiling her shears,
and fled, a week overpaid. Behind her back, when
she went to church, talk about wart-hogs in war-togs,
they called her Brothelhag, bartering sniggers,
and the sweat chilled on them in case she knew.

One lay awake at night sheeted in terror, when
the Hagglebroth bloomers billowing from the line
rose in binocular glory and loomed at his window
like a zeppelin. He left. They all left. Even
the glutted fly. Finally Mrs Hagglebroth herself
left, in a brand-new box sealed against sunlight.

So we have here the Hagglebroth effects. The souls
of miscellaneous gentlemen, welded to wicker chairs.
The fears of young men and the dread of old, potted
in antique brass. Several conscience racks, disguised
as beds. Connoisseur stuff, all of it. So come now,
ladies, you have your catalogues. . . . What am I bid?

IAIN CRICHTON SMITH

Old Woman

And she, being old, fed from a mashed plate
as an old mare might droop across a fence
to the dull pastures of its ignorance.
Her husband held her upright while he prayed

to God who is all-forgiving to send down
some angel somewhere who might land perhaps
in his foreign wings among the gradual crops.
She munched, half dead, blindly searching the spoon.

Outside, the grass was raging. There I sat
imprisoned in my pity and my shame
that men and women having suffered time
should sit in such a place, in such a state

and wished to be away, yes, to be far away
with athletes, heroes, Greeks or Roman men
who pushed their bitter spears into a vein
and would not spend an hour with such decay.

'Pray God', he said, 'we ask you, God,' he said.
The bowed back was quiet. I saw the teeth
tighten their grip around a delicate death.
And nothing moved within the knotted head

but only a few poor veins as one might see
vague wishless seaweed floating on a tide
of all the salty waters where had died
too many waves to mark two more or three.

Luss Village

Such walls, like honey, and the old are happy
in morphean air like gold-fish in a bowl.
Ripe roses trail their margins down a sleepy
mediaeval treatise on the slumbering soul.

And even the water, fabulously silent,
has no salt tales to tell us, nor makes jokes
about the yokel mountains, huge and patient,
that will not court her but read shadowy books.

A world so long departed! In the churchyard
the tilted tombs still gossip, and the leaves
of stony testaments are read by Richard,
Jean and Carol, pert among the sheaves

of unscythed meadows, while the noon day hums
with bees and water and the ghosts of psalms.

Two Girls Singing

It neither was the words nor yet the tune.
Any tune would have done and any words.
Any listener or no listener at all.

As nightingales in rocks or a child crooning
in its own world of strange awakening
or larks for no reason but themselves.

So on the bus through late November running
by yellow lights tormented, darkness falling,
the two girls sang for miles and miles together

and it wasn't the words or tune. It was the singing.
It was the human sweetness in that yellow,
the unpredicted voices of our kind.

The Witches

Coveys of black witches gather
at corners, closes.
Their thin red pointed noses
are in among the mash of scandal.

Poking red fires with
intense breath, hot as the imagined
rape riding the hot mind.
The real one was more moral

and more admirable because animal.
In an empty air they convene
their red, sad, envious, beaks. The clean
winter rubs them raw

in a terrible void, hissing
with tongues of winter fire.
Pity them, pity them. Dare
to ring them with your love.

The Cemetery Near Burns' Cottage

Tombs of the Covenanters nod together
grey heads and obstinate. They saw them come
the silver horsemen meditating murder
but stood there quietly to the beating drum
of God and psalm, the heart's immaculate order.

So now I see them as the churchyard turns
red in the evening light. They did not know
that moral milk turns sour, and something churns
inside the stony cask. This churchyard now
flickers with light, untameably with Burns,

the secret enemy within the stone,
the hand which even here stings its hot whip
in glittering rays from socketed bone to bone.
In such fixed Eden did his changing shape
unlock their teeth from what they'd bravely won.

The Temptation

Imagine, say, a mediaeval window
quietly painting grass from its studied green.
Imagine a monk or two soberly walking,
both gown and soul immaculately clean.
Also, behind them, a fine passage of birds
like a taste of Latin, a clear sip of Greek.
Imagine them walking like this, too quiet to speak.

And say you imagine it well, the hum of learning,
that queenless hive, a manuscript inlaid
with the whipped body's colours. (Say a sun
had gaily pierced a black devilish cloud.)
Imagine also a fine hush of prayer,

a library where God might be caught
dining perhaps on a Vergilian thought.

You might be tempted, yes, you might be tempted
till you remembered the draughts of cold rooms,
a sort of love gone wrong, a false devotion,
snarled horses smoking past in windy glooms,
and you might say yes: Yes, it was very well,
yes, there was something, but suppose a man
laughed at and burnt to a sacked autumn grain.

And also remember well the stake, the jeering
in a religious drizzle, while the calm
angels surrounded God at shining tables.
Directions glittered on a soldier's helm
The page was warm and green in monkish hands
but there, outside, a man was bent in two
to teach him that his arrows must fly true.

Lenin

In a chair of iron
sits coldly my image of Lenin,
that troubling man
'who never read a book for pleasure alone.'

The germ inside the sealed train
emerged, spread in wind and rain
into new minds in revolution
seeming more real than had been

for instance Dostoevsky. No, I can
romanticise no more that 'head of iron'
'the thought and will unalterably one'
'the word-doer', 'thunderer', 'the stone

179

rolling through clouds.' Simple to condemn
the unsymmetrical, simple to condone
that which oneself is not. By admiration
purge one's envy of unadult iron

when the true dialectic is to turn
in the infinitely complex, like a chain
we steadily burn through, steadily forge and burn
not to be dismissed in any poem

by admiration for the ruthless man
nor for the saint but for the moving on
into the endlessly various, real, human,
world which is no new era, shining dawn.

IAN HAMILTON FINLAY

Bedtime

So put your nightdress on
It is so white and long
And your sweet night-face
Put it on also please
It is the candle-flame
It is the flame above
Whose sweet shy shame
My love, I love, I love.

Black Tomintoul

To Scotland came the tall American
And went to stay on a little farm
Oh it was a Scotch farm set in the wild
A wee Scotch burn and a stoney field

She came to a corner, it was raining
And the little trees were all leaning in
This was Scotland the way she had thought of it
Care, not gravity, makes them lean
The rain falling Scotchly, Scotchly
And the hills that did not soar up but in

But most she looked at the bull so wild
She looked at the bull with the eyes of a child
Never in New York did she see such a bull
As this great Scotch one, Tomintoul
She called him secretly, the great Scotch bull

He was black all over, even for a bull
And oh he had such a lovely hide
She saw him follow one cow aside
Tell me, please, is that cow his bride?
No, they are all his lawful br-r-ride
There were twenty-four cows on the Scotch hillside

It was almost too much for the tall American girl
She watched him stand on his opposite hill
Black Tomintoul, and he always bellowed
But afterwards something in her was mellowed.

STEWART CONN

Todd

My father's white uncle became
Arthritic and testamental in
Lyrical stages. He held cardinal sin
Was misuse of horses, then any game

Won on the sabbath. A Clydesdale
To him was not bells and sugar or declension

From paddock, but primal extension
Of rock and soil. Thundered nail

Turned to sacred bolt. And each night
In the stable he would slaver and slave
At cracked hooves, or else save
Bowls of porridge for just the right

Beast. I remember I lied
To him once, about oats: then I felt
The brand of his loving tongue, the belt
Of his own horsey breath. But he died,

When the mechanised tractor came to pass.
Now I think of him neighing to some saint
In a simple heaven or, beyond complaint,
Leaning across a fence and munching grass.

The Clearing

Woodsmoke, sheer grapebloom, smears
The trunks of trees, tricks larches
Lilac, and as deftly clears.
Startlingly, among patches

Of sunlight, come glints
Of steel: the woodmen are at it
Early. Red-jerkined, gigantic
In quirk lighting, they flit

Under branches, make markings
Or, smirched, become blurs
Of themselves. Somewhere a dog barks.
Hand-saws spark, and sputter.

Breaking cover, a brood
Of partridges wheedles
Through charlock. Lopped wood,
Crippling down, sends needles

Showering. Blades whirr; logs are
Rolled and chained. Crushed
Brushwood leaks. Air
Is spiced with resin and sawdust.

Then they are gone, to the sound
Of singing. Where pathways join,
Fires flicker. And the ground
Is littered with huge and copper coins.

ROBIN FULTON

Clear Morning on a Hill

Shape comes with light. The hill
With clear edges becomes high;
Moss, with its own edges and tiny
Shadows, becomes what moss is.

A man, himself clear in the light,
Imagines hill upon hill upon hill,
Builds them from, shrinks them to
The one hill under his feet.

The light adds nothing but itself
Yet will make the hill simple
And heavy, the moss intricate,
Long after the man has carried
His unsteady hills away.

Gods

Between the sixth and the seventh days they came.

Myths, white-winged, infallible,
Struck tall fountains from the sea;
The goddess reclined on her shell; high tide
Laid dead dolphins on a mattress of weed;
At the resurrection of spring flowers a faun
Fathered his shadow with multitudinous spawn.

After it all, when the legend of trees had withered
And the wind's lawless fingers had ripped the leaves,
We came on the seventh day to the naked woods
Expecting vestals raped by their drunk gods
And corn-kings nailed on their trees. By dawn
We had found nothing but certain articles of sin.

Another history of gods was about to begin.

D. M. BLACK

The Red Judge

We shut the red judge in a bronze jar
—By 'we', meaning myself and the black judge—
And there was peace, for a time. You can have enough
Yowling from certain justices. The jar
We buried (pitching and swelling like the tough
Membrane of an unshelled egg) on the Calton Hill.
And there was peace, for a time. My friend the black
Judge was keen on whisky, and I kept
Within earshot of sobriety only by drinking
Slow ciders, and pretending
Unfelt absorption in the repetitive beer-mats. It was a kind of
Vibration we noticed first—hard to tell

Whether we heard it or were shaken by,
Whether the tumblers quivered or our minds. It grew
To a thick thudding, and an occasional creak
Like a nearby axle, but as it were
Without the sense of 'nearby' – The hard flag-
stones wriggled slightly under the taut linoleum.
I supported the black judge to the nearest door
– Detached his clutched glass for the protesting barman –
And propped him against a bus-stop. Maybe
It was only a pneumatic drill mating at Queen Street,
Or an impotent motor-bike – the sounds grew harsher:
My gestures stopped a 24 that spat
Some eleventh commandment out of its sober driver,
But I was more conscious of the rocking walls,
The pavement's shrugging off its granite kerb . . .

Quite suddenly the night was still: the cracks
In the roadway rested, and the tenements
Of Rose Street stood inscrutable as always. The black judge
Snored at his post. And all around
The bright blood filled the gutters, overflowed
The window-sills and door-steps, soaked my anyway
Inadequate shoes, and there was a sound of cheering
Faintly and everywhere, and the Red Judge walked
O thirty feet high and scarlet towards our stop.

The Black Judge Debonair

A blonde with great legendary eyes flew down,
Lit nestling on the bar-stool. I
Ordered her a cursory martini and
Turned to resume our talk, but the dark judge was
Already at her other wing, faking profound
Fellow-feeling.

     Relish for the pub's decor,
Delight in the plosive froth, and a gleaming wit

About fishnet stockings brought him close to the bull's-eye.
Her giggling and readjustment on the stool
Sighted his aim.

       And it was not closing time
That took them from the pub, and led them down
To the open allotment gardens, under the grey
Starlight.

       As he undid her out of zips
And hooks the night
Was innumerably still. He slipped off his own
Clothes and laid her down along the verge,
And all laughter was gone from her features. After a certain point
The inadequacy of facial expression is best
Masked altogether. He stood back
To admire his work, God on a seventh day
Hanging above action. And saw the red
Judge's grin absent from the factual target.

That calm godlikeness in the upper air
Shatters, and is more a hawk that
Stoops furiously onto its simple prey.

GLOSSARY

(No attempt has been made to standardise the spelling used by poets of different generations, but all variants encountered in the text are given.)

ablow	below
abraid	abroad, about
abune	above
ae	one, only
agley	apart
aiblins	maybe, perhaps
aik	oak
aince	once
air	early
airms	arms
airn	iron
airtless	directionless
Albannach	belonging to Alba, the Pictish and Gaelic name of Scotland
albeid	although
anerlie	only
ase	ash
auld	old
auld-farrant	old-fashioned
auntran, antrin	occasional
a wee thing	a bit
ay	yes
aye	always
ayebydan	everlasting
ayont	beyond
back-lands	sunless tenement houses
baffies	slippers
bairdie	beardy (beaver)
bairn	child
bairnkie	small child
balas	precious stones

ballant	ballad
bane-cauld	bone-cold
banker	hewing-table
bellochin	bellowing
ben	inside
bent	grassland
bield	shelter
bien	snug
bienlie	comfortable
biggin	building
binnae	except
birss	sharp
blads	pages
blate	bashful
blee	complexion
blethers	nonsensical chatter
bluffert	a gust (of wind)
bodach	an old man
bogle	evil spirit
boussum	gracious
braw	well-looking
breer	sprouting corn
breist	breast
brenn	burn
brou	brow
broukit	neglected
bruckle	brittle
brunt	burnt
bunesaid	above said
buss	bush
byde	to remain, live
bydand	waiting
caa	call
cailleach	the old hag of storm and winter
cantie	cheerful
cantilie	cheerfully
caunel	candle

causeys	cobble-stones
causie	crown of the road
chafts	jaws
chalmer	room
chappan	striking
chitterin	shivering
chowks	cheeks
chyld	man
clanjamfrie	collection of people
Clarach	strait between Raasay and Skye
clatt neeps	thin out turnips with a hoe
clorty	dirty
clour	an upset
coorse	coarse
corp	body
crack	conversation
craig	throat
crammasy, crammasie	crimson
creashy	greasy
creelfu	basketful
creepies	three-legged stools
crined	shrunk
crines	shrivels
crousie	convivial
crozie	fawning, sycophantic
cruach	heap, stack, mountain
daff	joke
darg	regular labour
dauds	lumps, bits
daw	dawn
dern	hidden
ding	a stroke
dinged	struck down
disjaskit	disarrayed
doitit	crack-brained
dotterel	dotard
douce	sweet, proper

dourlie	stubbornly
dowf	spiritless
dowp	haunch
dozie	stupefied
dree	endure
dreich	dull
droolie	slobbering
droukit	soaked
drouths	drunks
drowie	damp
drumlie	muddy
duds	rags
dule	sorrow, grief
dullyart	of a dirty colour
dune	exhausted
dwaiblan	lurching infirmly
dwaiblie	infirm
dwaum	swoon, day-dream
dwine	to decline
ee	eye
een	eyes
eild	age
elbucks	elbows
Embro	Edinburgh
eneuch	enough
fairlie	surely
fankl't, fangled	tangled
fash	to bother
faur owr	much too
feckless	feeble
fegs	faith (oath)
feiman	in violent heat and commotion
fell	strange
fend	find
ferlie	a wonder, marvel
ferm-toun	farm buildings
flaught	crowd

fleggin	frightening
flirn	to twist
flume	steam, flood
fog	moss
forbye	besides
forcochen, forfeuchan	exhausted
fou	full
fousome	disgusting
fowk	fold
fowr airts	four points of the compass
fozie	soiled, diseased
fraeth	mist
fremd	foreign
frith	firth
fyled	soiled
gangrel	vagrant
gant	gape, yawn
gars	makes
gash	to prattle
geck	dupe
gentrice	gentleness
gesserant	gleaming metallically, like armour
ghaist	ghost
gib	tom-cat
gin	if
girn	to snare, a snare
girn	to grouse, complain
glack	pass
glauman	gleaming through mist
glaumerie	enchantment
glaur	dirt, mud
gled	hawk
gleg	acute, quick
gleid	fire
glinkan	winking
glisk	glimpse, gleam
gloamin	twilight

glower	to scowl
glunch	to gape
goun	gown
gowd	gold
gowden	golden
gowdie	jewel
gowf	golf
Gowf, The	a pub in Edinburgh
gowk	cuckoo, fool
gowkit	glanced stupidly
greens	lawns
greet, greit	to weep, complain
grein	yearn, long for
gruntles	snouts
guff	belch
gyte	mad
haar	mist from the sea
haill	whole
hairst	harvest
hamewith	homewards
hap	wrap
hapt	covered
hauf-mutchkin	half bottle of whisky
heeze	rear
heich	high
heicht	height
heid	head
het	hot
heud	to hold
hidderie hetterie	hither and thither
hike	to fetch
hine	far off
hing	to hang
hinny	honey
hint	behind
hirplan	limping
hotteran	simmering

houlit	howled
hous-rig	house roof
howdumbdeid	dead of night
howe, howie	hollow
Howe-hollow	Mearns, Kincardineshire
howf	pub, haunt
hudder	to huddle
huggerin	gathering in folds
hunder	hundred
hurdies	buttocks
hyne	few
ilk	each
ilka	every
in-ben	within
ingans	onions
ir	or
jaggan	pricking
jake	same as 'reid-biddie'
jing-bang	the whole lot
jizzen	childbirth
kaain	driving
kail-pat	soup-pot
keek	to peep
keen	to wail
ken	to know
kent	known
kirkyairdielike	funereal
kist	chest
kittl't	tickled
knock	clock
kye	cows
laich	low
laigh	hollow
laigh-boutit	bowed low
laird	landowner
land	tenement house

lanesome	lonely
lave	remainder
laverock	lark (see 'reek')
lawlie	downcast
lea	to leave
leal	loyal
leaman	flaming
lees	shelter
lent-lillies	daffodils
leuch	laughed
lift, luft	sky
liggan	lying
linn	waterfall
lippen	to listen
loesome	loveable
loom-bund	fog-bound
loon	fellow
lour	to loom
lourd	heavy
lown	quiet
lowp	to leap
lowsing-time	time to stop work
luely	softly
lugs	ears
lush-raip	a blow that rips open
Machar	seaside pasture
Mahoun	Mahommed (i.e. the Devil)
makar	poet
march	boundary
Mary's Bath-tub	traditionally, Mary, Queen of Scots' Bath House (which is obviously nonsense, but it is called so)
mappamound	atlas
maun	must
meat	food
mell	to mix
mell	mason's mallet

mensefu	sensible
merchless	boundless
midden	dunghill
mirk	darkness
mixter-maxter	jumbled
mouls	clods
mousewabs	cobwebs
Mownth	the Grampian range
mowdie-man	molecatcher
mowdie-worps	moles
muckle	great, big
muin, mune, müne	moon
murns	mourns
mynd	to remember
nebstous	nostrils
neeps	turnips
nicht	night
nor-aist	north-east
ochtither	anything else
oe	grandchild
O-hone-a-ree!	Alas!
onding	fall of rain, or snow
onie	any
oorie	chill, bleak
or	until
ourie	cold, wet
outby	just outside
outland	outcast
owr, owre, ower	over, about
owrecome	the refrain of a song
owrehailan	overwhelming
owsen	oxen
park	field
partan-creels	crab-baskets
pat	pot
Pate	Peter

pechin, pechan	panting
pend	close arch
pleu	plough
poke	pocket
pouther't	powdered
pree	to taste, experience, make proof of
purtith	poverty
quaich	to scream loudly
quait	quiet
racks	caves
raivan	raving
ramsh	fiery (of spirits)
rare	choice
rauchan	plaid
rax	to reach
redds up	cleans up
reek	smoke ('nae reek i' the laverock's hoose'—it was a dark and stormy night)
reeshlit	rustled
reid	red
reid-biddie	methylated spirits mixed with cheap wine
reivers	rustlers, thieves
rickle	skeletal stack
rigg	ridge, furrow
roose	praise
rouch, reuch	rough
rouk	fog, mist
rowin	rolling
rowtan	snoring
runt	stump
rutes	roots
sanct	saint
saut	salt
saw	sow

scart	to scratch
scaud	scald
schere	brilliant
sclate	slate
sclent	slant, glint
scraich	to shriek
screwtap chasers	screwtop bottles of beer
scrieve	to write
scrievin	writing
scrievit	written
scunner, sconner	to disgust
sea-maw	seagull (lit. 'sea-stomach')
secks	sacks
seilfu	blissful
shennachies	storytellers
shilpet	sickly
shitten	foul
shuinn	shoes
sic	such
siccar	sure
skail	to disperse, empty
skaith	harm, wound
skalrag	tatterdemalion
skelf	small piece of stone or wood
skinklan	shining
skirl	to scream
skuddert	skidded
slee	cunning, sly
sleek	sleet, snow
smairged	bedaubed
smochteran	choking
smool'd	glided softly
smoored, smored, smoorit	smothered
snell	keen
sniftert	snuffled
snog	snug
snorled	ravelled
sodger	soldier

sonsie	plump
soom	to swim
spaul	limb, back
speils	climbs
stand o blacks	a suit of black clothes
stang	pang, sting
stark	strong
starn	star
steekit	shut
steer	to stir
steir	fat
stibble	stubble
stieve	stiff
stour	dust
strae	straw
strampin	vigorously tramping
strand	beach
strappin	sturdy
stravaig	to wander
streel	urine
swack	to strike violently
swaiver	to move aimlessly
swaw	wave
sweirness	laziness
sweirt	reluctant
swither	flurry
tae	too
taiglit, taigled	tangled
t'ane	the one
tattie-dulie	scarecrow
tattie-howk	potato lifting
tene	sorrow
tenty o' them	aware of them
thaikit	thatched
thir	these
thirled	tied, enslaved
thole	to endure

thon	yonder
thrang	crowd, busy
thrapple	throat
threep	to converse
threeps	harangues
timber-sark	wooden shirt (i.e. coffin)
timmer	wooden
tine	to lose
tinks	tinkers
tint	lost
Tir-nan-Og	Paradise (pronounced 'cheer-nan-og')
tither	the other
toom	empty
touzie	tousled
tramorts	corpses
trauchlit	worn down with labour
twal	twelve
tykes	dogs
ugsome	frightful
unco	strange, peculiar
undemous	immeasurable
unrazit	unshaven
unsocht	unsought
unsteek	open
vricht	carpenter
waa	wall
wae	sorrowful
walliecoat	waistcoat
wames	stomachs
wan	pale
wanchancy	unlucky
warsslan	struggling
watergaw	rainbow
wauken	awake
waukrife hour	time for waking up

waur	worse
wecht	weight
weet	wet
weil-snod	well looked after
weird	fate
weirdless	fateless
wersh	tasteless, insipid
westlins	westering
whartil	whereto
whaups	curlews
wheen	a number
wheesht	be quiet
while	until
whiles	at times
whusslit	whistled
widdreme	scene of chaos, confusion
winnockie	windowy (i.e. full of holes)
wir	our
wirricou	wild
wrack	vengeance, sea-weed
wreist	to fidget
wreithes	swathes of mist or fog
wud	furious, mad
yalla	yellow
yammerin	talking complainingly
Yerl Marischal	Earl Marshal of Scotland
yestreen	last night
yett	gate
yill	ale
yirdy	earthy
yirked	jerked
yow-trummle	cold spell after the July shearing when the ewes, being clipped, shiver
yowden-druft	snow driven by the wind
yowe-hoast	a cough like a sick ewe's